IRAQ
RECONSTRUCTION
AND FUTURE ROLE

IRAQ
RECONSTRUCTION AND FUTURE ROLE

THE EMIRATES CENTER FOR STRATEGIC STUDIES AND RESEARCH

THE EMIRATES CENTER FOR STRATEGIC STUDIES AND RESEARCH

The Emirates Center for Strategic Studies and Research (ECSSR) is an independent research institution dedicated to the promotion of professional studies and educational excellence in the UAE, the Gulf and the Arab world. Since its establishment in Abu Dhabi in 1994, ECSSR has served as a focal point for scholarship on political, economic and social matters. Indeed, ECSSR is at the forefront of analysis and commentary on Arab affairs.

The Center seeks to provide a forum for the scholarly exchange of ideas by hosting conferences and symposia, organizing workshops, sponsoring a lecture series and publishing original and translated books and research papers. ECSSR also has an active fellowship and grant program for the writing of scholarly books and for the translation into Arabic of work relevant to the Center's mission. Moreover, ECSSR has a large library including rare and specialized holdings, and a state-of-the-art technology center, which has developed an award-winning website that is a unique and comprehensive source of information on the Gulf.

Through these and other activities, ECSSR aspires to engage in mutually beneficial professional endeavors with comparable institutions worldwide, and to contribute to the general educational and scientific development of the UAE.

First published in 2004 by
The Emirates Center for Strategic Studies and Research
PO Box 4567, Abu Dhabi, United Arab Emirates

E-mail: pubdis@ecssr.ac.ae
pubdis@ecssr.com

Website: http://www.ecssr.ac.ae
http://www.ecssr.com

ISBN 9948-00-639-9 hardback edition

ISBN 9948-00-638-0 paperback edition

CONTENTS

FIGURES AND TABLES

ABBREVIATIONS AND ACRONYMS

ADCO	Abu Dhabi Company for Onshore Oil Operations
ADM	Assyrian Democratic Movement
ADNOC	Abu Dhabi National Oil Company
bcm/y	Billion cubic meters per year
bd	Barrels per day
bn	Billion
Centcom	Central Command
CERA	Cambridge Energy Research Associates
CPA	Coalition Provisional Authority
DPC	Development and Production Contracts
GCC	Gulf Cooperation Council
IAEA	International Atomic Energy Agency
IFLB	Islamic Front for the Liberation of Bahrain
IIP	Iraqi Islamic Party
ILA	Iraq Liberation Act
IMIK	Islamic Movement of Iraqi Kurdistan
INA	Iraq National Accord
INC	Iraqi National Congress
INF	Iraqi National Front
INM	Iraqi National Movement
INOC	Iraq National Oil Company
IOC	International Oil Company
JODCO	Japan Offshore Development Company
KBR	Kellogg Brown and Root
KDP	Kurdistan Democratic Party
KLA	Kosovo Liberation Army
KPC	Kuwait Petroleum Company
LNG	Liquefied Natural Gas
mbd	Million barrels per day
MCM	Movement for Constitutional Monarchy
MEES	Middle East Economic Survey
MIT	Massachusetts Institute of Technology
NATO	North Atlantic Treaty Organization

NPT	Treaty on the Non-Proliferation of Nuclear Weapons
OPEC	Organization of Petroleum Exporting Countries
OSA	Operating Service Agreements
PKK	Kurdish Worker's Party
PSC	Production Sharing Contracts
PUK	Patriotic Union of Kurdistan
SCIRI	Supreme Council for the Islamic Revolution in Iraq
SEC	Securities and Exchange Commission
SFOR	Stabilization Force
SOMO	State and Marketing Organization (Iraq)
SPC	Supreme Petroleum Council
UAE	United Arab Emirates
UK	United Kingdom
UN	United Nations
UNMIK	UN Interim Administration in Kosovo
UNMOVIC	UN Monitoring, Verification and Inspection Commission
US	United States
USACE	US Army Corps of Engineers
USAID	US Agency for International Development
WMD	Weapons of Mass Destruction
ZADCO	Zakum Development Company

Iraq has always been a country whose activities and exploits have impacted on all its neighbors, especially the countries of the Arabian Gulf. Through history, it has been both friend and foe, and through the last decades of Saddam Hussein's reign, it has elicited much concern.

The March 2003 war in Iraq sparked heated debate, first concerning its legitimacy, then its unfolding and now its aftermath. There is little doubt that it is in the interests of the Iraqis, the Coalition Forces, the broader international community and Iraq's neighbors that peace and stability is reached and maintained in Iraq, through a system chosen by its people.

Iraq is a country whose natural wealth, if optimally exploited, can bring great benefit to the Iraqi people. It is also a country that can contribute strongly to regional stability and economic development. A stable Iraq under a legitimate and stable government has the potential to be a positive force in the Middle East. Yet, developments in the aftermath of the war do not provide clear indications that the route Iraq is following will result in success—that is, a unified Iraq, living at peace with itself and its neighbors, using its full capacity for economic recovery and its goodwill for regional prosperity.

Much concern exists around the vested interests in the outcome of the Iraqi war. While the United States wants to see a democratic Iraq under a US-friendly government, it cannot be up to the US to determine the final shape of the Iraqi political system or its economic relations. Iraq's neighbors, particularly in the Gulf, have the concern that a politically unstable Iraq may leak instability over its borders. They also have the added concern of how to accommodate a stable and strong Iraq as an oil producer whose impact on OPEC cannot be underestimated. Iraq's neighbors to the east and north, Iran and Syria respectively, have their own internal stability and regional ambitions to consider. Finally, Iran's professed nuclearization is of much concern to the region in particular and to the broader international community in general. No doubt, the route that Iran chooses to take on the issue of nuclear weapons will have a major impact on any future scenario in the region.

Internally, Iraqis themselves also have an enormous responsibility for the reconstruction and development of Iraq. Factionalism and divisiveness will no doubt lead to instability, vulnerability and economic demise. It is in the interests of the Iraqi people that all effort be made to support those Iraqi institutions already established, the local authority councils and the Iraqi police in order to provide security for the reconstruction of their country.

It is because the future of Iraq is of such importance to the Middle East region and the Arabian Gulf in particular that the Emirates Center for Strategic Studies and Research (ECSSR) hosted a series of lectures and a symposium entitled "Iraq: Reconstruction and Future Role," in Abu Dhabi, on September 14–15, 2003. Specialists in the field of Iraqi politics, development and energy were invited to share their views on the war, its aftermath and possible scenarios for the future.

This volume is a valuable collection of these expert views. It provides strategic perspectives on the important subjects of "Iraqi Reconstruction and Regional Security," "Anti-Americanism and the

Future of the US–Iraq Relationship," "Political Scenarios in Post-War Iraq," "Islamist Politics in Iraq after the Fall of Saddam" and "Iraq in a New Map of Oil Supplies."

ECSSR would like to take this opportunity to thank the authors for their valuable contributions. A word of thanks is also extended to ECSSR editor Deborah Watson for coordinating the publication of this book.

Jamal S. Al Suwaidi, Ph.D.
Director General
ECSSR

Section 1

INTRODUCTION

Agents of Change in the New Iraq

Most momentous events in history are subject to heated debate, widely differing opinions and conflicting evaluations.* Consensus is seldom reached while the occurrence in question is still unfolding and frequently not even once the episode is concluded.

As an event of significance in modern history, the 2003 war in Iraq is a subject that elicits a variety of views and evokes deep emotions. While the legitimacy of the war remains open to question, attention has largely shifted from the debates in the international arena to developments inside Iraq itself.

The one area where consensus can be found is that all involved, and even those who are not, desire to see a peaceful Iraq, playing its rightful role among the community of nations, a territorially intact Iraq and an Iraq for all Iraqis. As such, the two principal areas of focus are Iraqi security and reconstruction.

---

* This introduction is based on the contents of papers presented in the ECSSR Lecture Series and at the ECSSR symposium entitled "Iraq: Reconstruction and Future Role".

On the issue of security, there are divergent views on how well the coalition forces are moving from making war to creating peace. The US-led occupation authority – the Coalition Provisional Authority (CPA) – is facing mounting resistance from factions within Iraq, reportedly supported by external elements. The motivation for such resistance appears to vary from the establishment of an Islamic state, the restoration of the former regime, opposition to foreign presence in Iraq and even the difficulty that the CPA is encountering with the instauration of civilian services.

Despite the upheaval inside Iraq at present, there are those who would argue that the CPA is making progress with security and stability. The establishment of the Iraqi Governing Council in July 2003 may be seen as a significant step towards Iraqi self-rule. This is especially remarkable in a country where the almost immediate collapse of the state after the March 2003 invasion was the clearest manifestation of the institutional weakness of the Iraqi governing structure under the decades of Saddam Hussein's regime. Foundations have to be laid upon which to build political structures and viable state institutions that can sustain a government elected by Iraqis.

In his chapter entitled, "Iraqi Reconstruction and Regional Security," Dr. Patrick Clawson mentions that polls indicate considerable support in Baghdad for the Governing Council as well as strong misgivings at continued foreign presence in Iraq. According to Dr. Kenneth Katzman, in his chapter entitled "Political Scenarios in Post-War Iraq," the Governing Council, although not a cohesive block, includes exiles and non-exiles that generally want a liberal democracy and would be considered pro-US.

[4]

However, the significant lesson to learn from experiences of democracy in countries of the Former Soviet Union and failed states is the need to first establish the rule of law and create vigorous civil society institutions. No doubt, the way to reduce anti-American sentiment in Iraq is to have Iraqis in charge of a new government as soon as possible. Yet, the speed with which this is achieved needs to be carefully determined. In Clawson's view, haste in handing over sovereignty would result in an interim government or premature elections which would likely bring well-organized exiles into power.

In his chapter, Katzman provides considerable detail on the various factions within the Iraqi political system. The current Governing Council reflects the various groupings in Iraqi politics, including some formerly in exile, as well as prominent Iraqis. To some, the appointment of individuals based on representational criteria as opposed to merit is an issue of contention, while others maintain that this is the only way to make all stakeholders accountable. The Governing Council has appointed a 25-member Cabinet as well as a 25-member commission which has drafted the new Iraqi constitution.

However, in her chapter entitled "Checking the Rising Tide: Anti-Americanism in Iraq and the Future of the US–Iraq Relationship," Dr. Bathsheba Crocker states that one of the concerns is that the precise authority and accountability of the Council have not been defined, thus affecting its legitimacy. The extent to which the new Iraqi institutions are perceived by Iraqis themselves as being truly representative of the Iraqi people and their national interests will be a strong determinant in the success of these institutions. Crocker maintains that the US must not be seen to predetermine how Iraq will look, what government it will have and what external relations it will enjoy. This would be a recipe for long-term failure in Iraq and in US–Iraqi relations.

The US strategic objective is the establishment of a stable democratic government in Iraq. However, its concern is that in any political system the Shiite majority will prevail. This raises anxiety of an Islamist government in the mould of the one that holds sway in neighboring Iran—a system wholly unacceptable to the US. Katzman maintains that it is almost inevitable that Shiite Islamist parties will achieve political dominance in Iraq. They have a well-developed leadership and are able to mobilize large numbers of Iraqis in a show of political strength.

Crocker also supports the view of the likely dominance of the Iraqi Shiites and states that their political power is a reality that the US has to face. A positive approach by the US would be to secure important relationships with moderate Shiites in Iraq in order to contain the extremist elements. It is an encouraging indicator that Iraqi Shiites have worked successfully with the Sunnis and the Kurds in Iraq, and have called for the establishment of an Islamic democracy. Moreover, the Iraqi Shiites have frequently declared their independence from their eastern neighbors.

Indeed, in his chapter entitled "Islamist Politics in Iraq after the Fall of Saddam," Graham Fuller maintains that the mere fact of being Shia does not imply that Iraqi Shiites wish to have an Islamic state in which clerics rule, as in Iran. In fact, the Iranian system as first established by Ayatollah Khomeini was a considerable innovation in Shiite history, not accepted by all Shiite clerics by any means. Fuller also comments that sectarianism is not the only foundation of Iraqi political and social organization. Prior to Saddam Hussein's policy of "divide and rule," Iraqis lived, worked and even married across sectarian lines. However, the legacy of decades of Baath rule, especially under Saddam, is a society in which sectarian divisions and rivalries have become entrenched and will form the key vehicle for political rivalry. There is, nevertheless, the possibility that in the long term Iraqi politics will normalize and demonstrate other social patterns of organization. For the present, there is little doubt that the Iraqi Shia will hold political sway, despite the factionalism manifest in Iraq at present.

An Iraq, where the strongest, if not the only, political voice will be Shia will certainly impact on relations with the Arabian Gulf and the broader Middle East. According to Fuller, a Shia Iraq may lend strength to demands from Shia minorities in some Gulf states, impact on the traditional relations of Iran with Syria and Lebanon, and move the Shia fulcrum from Qom, the center of clerical rule in Iran, back to the holy cities of Najaf and Karbala, prominent traditional centers of Shia theology in Iraq.

On the subject of the defense of Iraq, factors other than internal dynamics will affect the extent to which the US will rebuild the Iraqi army—pertinently, the security environment in the Arabian Gulf. According to Clawson, two principal scenarios could unfold in the Gulf region: one, a peaceful environment of cooperation and progress that will see a reduction in defense expenditure and a greater focus on trade and economic development; two, an environment of insecurity and tension hinging mainly on the decision Iran takes concerning its nuclear development. Should Iran persist in the development of nuclear weapons, this is likely to draw the Gulf countries into a race for military modernization, and drive Iraq to build a huge modern army and possibly try to acquire its own nuclear capability. The latter scenario will clearly impact on the availability of resources that would otherwise be directed towards socio-economic growth.

Notwithstanding future regional scenarios or perhaps because of them, it is critical for the CPA that security and stability be established as soon as possible, since security is the backbone for US success in Iraq. The US will retain a responsibility for the defense of Iraq, for as long as Iraq does not have its own effective defense force. Thus, Katzman maintains, there is strong motivation to develop an effective Iraqi police to manage internal instability, freeing the US/Coalition forces to defend the Iraqi borders against possible external threats or infiltration. Clawson mentions that progress in this sphere is occurring with the rebuilding of the Iraqi police and the establishment of local authority councils in 60 cities.

Since August 2003, negotiations have also gained momentum to try to establish a UN-authorized peacekeeping force in Iraq. There are many arguments supporting the view held by Crocker that there is a need for a greater UN role in Iraq, not least to reduce the determination of the US to dominate the situation in the country. Despite the fact that several nations do have troops in Iraq, several of the large countries are waiting for a UN resolution endorsing such a mission. However, one of the factors that such a decision could be contingent upon would be the downscaling of US authority in Iraq, which the US appears reluctant to countenance.

Nevertheless, according to Katzman, the growing resistance and escalating occupation costs may compel the US Administration to give up some of its control in exchange for spreading the burden of peacekeeping. Meanwhile, Clawson comments that the UN appears to be reluctant to risk more than a few members in Iraq. This reluctance may seriously curtail its role in the stability and reconstruction of the country, still leaving most of the decisions and the action to the US. He argues in his chapter that what Iraq needs is not more foreign troops, but rather specialist skills in basic services like policing and repair of rudimentary machinery, skills that could better be provided by countries other than the US.

Internal security and stability are the *sine qua non* of Iraqi reconstruction. This is not to say that reconstruction has not been occurring. In fact, Clawson maintains that depending on the standard of measurement used, the reconstruction of Iraq can be deemed as proceeding satisfactorily. Compared with Kosovo and Bosnia, for example, Iraq has achieved more in peace-building and reconstruction efforts in less time. The informal sector is strengthening, especially since the CPA abolished taxes, imports are flooding into Iraq at far lower prices than before and trade is flourishing.

Furthermore, the amount of financial aid being given to Iraq far exceeds what other countries are receiving in aid. Aid to Pakistan is less than one percent of what is proposed for Iraq. This may well be one of the strongest indicators of the desire of the US to succeed in Iraq. However, in terms of foreign capital entering the country, large international investors place great onus on the security of their investment. While physical security is important, institutional stability and transparency are also strong investor requirements.

Although some like Clawson maintain that reconstruction in Iraq is progressing reasonably well, Crocker maintains that the slow pace of provision of basic facilities, like electricity and water, may be creating the impression that the US is either unable or unwilling to help Iraqis rebuild their country. The rumors persist that the US is in Iraq solely to control Iraqi oil production.

However, in her chapter entitled "Iraq in a New Map of Oil Supplies: Implications for Other Gulf Oil Producers," Ms. Vera de Ladoucette maintains that, while it is true that American companies lead the restoration of Iraq's production capacity, first term contracts for lifting Iraqi crude have been awarded to European and Asian companies as much as to American. There is a dire need to restore surface capacity and the reservoirs that were damaged. Continued sabotage of the infrastructure exacerbates the problem and delays reconstruction. According to de Ladoucette, the situation surrounding the oil industry will not improve much before 2007. Even this scenario is dependent on political stabilization, as the large oil companies have made it clear that they seek stabilization and a legitimate Iraqi government that has the authority and longevity to sign long-term agreements. They also seek clarity on Iraqi fiscal plans.

The issue of oil quotas is perhaps more central than uncertainty about future production levels. De Ladoucette maintains that there is increased capacity in Algeria, Libya and the United Arab Emirates. Iran has argued that reserves should be the determining factor in capacity and has recently declared increased reserves. Nevertheless, members of the Organization of Petroleum Exporting Countries (OPEC) have been losing market share and will likely continue to lose market share until 2007. With the opening of Iraq's oil industry, companies will be looking in that direction for allocation of funds and competition will increase. OPEC will have to revisit its oil strategy.

It is therefore clear, that from a political, economic and social perspective, what happens in Iraq will have to be closely watched by the countries in the Gulf region and the broader Middle East. In the words of Dr. Crocker: "If Iraq becomes a stable, prosperous democracy, it could exert a powerful and positive influence on the region. However, if Iraq descends into chaos, the consequences would be disastrous." It is certain that events in Iraq will impact on its neighbors. What needs to be determined by the latter is how much that impact can be optimized or mitigated and how it can best be managed.

CURRENT DEVELOPMENTS

1

Iraqi Reconstruction and Regional Security

Patrick Clawson

T he thesis of this chapter can be readily summarized—the reconstruction of Iraq is going well by many standards, but not by the high expectations created pre-war. Proposals for a radically different approach to the reconstruction of Iraq are generally misconceived; in particular, a broader international role would do little to help the Iraqi people.

The most appropriate approach is for the United States (US) to take the lead in handing power over to the Iraqi people as soon as new institutions can be created. Nevertheless, the United States will still have to help for the foreseeable future in the defense of Iraq.

Moreover, there is the worrying possibility that instead of a benign security environment in which militaries everywhere can be phased down, the Arab Gulf states, including Iraq, will face a nuclear-armed Iran, which would create a difficult security situation requiring strong militaries and an active US security presence.

Judging Iraqi Reconstruction: By What Standard?

Much of the difference about how well reconstruction is going in Iraq comes from disagreements about what standard to use to judge the progress. Let us assess how well things are going in Iraq compared to several different standards.

By the standards of recent international interventions, things in Iraq are going quite well. In Kosovo and Bosnia, which are heralded as success stories, physical reconstruction has gone slower and been subject to many complaints about corruption and cronyism. Political progress has been even slower than physical reconstruction, with the United Nations still in charge, overriding locals.

Consider Kosovo. In January 2003, more than three and half years after assuming control over the civil administration of Kosovo, the United Nations Interim Administration in Kosovo (UNMIK) estimated that international civil servants still held 40 percent of the "competencies" in Kosovo, which is a UN term for positions of authority.[1] The target for 2003 was to reduce this share to 20 percent. As for the relationship among ethno-religious groups in Kosovo, there has been no progress toward reconciliation between the Serbian and Albanian populations of Kosovo or between the Kosovars and Serbia. Indeed, UNMIK's goal is simply peaceful coexistence, not reconciliation. In other words, the UN-run administration is proving to be a long-term proposition with no appreciable impact on reducing hostilities between the parties. As for security, the UN-led forces in post-war Kosovo confronted much the same sort of disorder and security problems that have plagued the US-led forces in post-war Iraq, even though one might have thought that the situation in Kosovo would be relatively simple since nearly all the local population favored the UN-led war. However, there emerged in fact a bitter split among the locals about

[14]

who would take power and whether to punish past collaborators. Faced with attacks by the Kosovo Liberation Army (KLA) – a loose collection of secretive paramilitary bands – UNMIK moved slowly, not making much progress in its first year.

In Bosnia, the UN-led effort dates back to 1995, which was the year of the Dayton Peace Agreement; eight years later, the international community is still actively involved in the running of the country. In 1995, the Secretary General appointed a High Representative (initially, Carl Bildt) and the North Atlantic Treaty Organization (NATO) sent in a force which came to be known as the Stabilization Force (SFOR). Bildt himself evaluated the record of SFOR and the High Representative to be "a mixed success" because "instead of a gradual transfer of more and more responsibilities to the institutions and parties of Bosnia itself, the consolidation period [1997–1998] has seen a gradual increase in the powers and functions of the international community in the country."[2] As in Kosovo, the record in Bosnia six months after the war was little better – and arguably worse – than in Iraq six months after that war.

The cynic might say that the Balkan UN experience is judged a success only because so many are involved that none wish to acknowledge their failures, whereas the US–Iraq experience is judged a failure because so many wish to criticize the United States. That suggests the United States might be politically wise to hand over responsibility to the UN, not because the UN could do any better than the United States but because the hand-over would quiet the international critics.

Another way to judge the Iraq reconstruction is by the standards of history, specifically the events after World War II. In fact, the reconstruction of Iraq is proceeding quicker than did the post-1945 reconstruction. The first year after the end of World War II saw declining living standards across the war-torn areas of Europe and Asia; indeed, the continuing serious economic problems were what led to the Marshall Plan, which only began more than three years after the war ended. As for political stabilization, it proceeded even slower with communist advances across Europe and Asia in previously free countries like Czechoslovakia and Poland as well as in huge countries such as China. Indeed, three years after the end of the war, the West almost lost Italy and France to Soviet advances. In the occupied countries, political progress was painfully slow; ten years after the war, there was still deep skepticism about whether Japan and Germany would be enduring democracies.

Yet another standard by which to judge the Iraq reconstruction is the standard of recent Iraqi history. By that standard as well, the reconstruction is going rather well. The reality of twenty years of war is that Iraq's infrastructure is worn out, requiring complete rebuilding. It is therefore hardly surprising that the infrastructure has continued to deteriorate despite the quick fixes of the coalition; real improvement must wait until new facilities can be built. The political scene is even worse. Thirty-five years of Baathist rule have left Iraqis without the experience of democracy and free enterprise. They lack experience with initiative, power sharing and compromise, all of which are essential to a functioning democratic, market economy.

On the security front, the situation in Iraq today is vastly better than during the years of Saddam's rule. During the last twenty years of war and accelerated terror, 400,000 Iraqis may have died from political violence, between the genocide against the Kurds, the senseless war against Iran, the brutal suppression of the 1991 uprisings, and the continuing killings of political opponents. Mass graves dot the country. The death rate from Saddam's slaughter was well in excess of the current problems. It is striking how many who now rush to deplore the current instability in Iraq were silent during all the years of Saddam's brutality. Indeed, many remain silent to this day about the reality of mass graves. The question must be asked: if these critics refuse to speak about the Saddam-era mass graves but object to the many fewer now dying, are their real concerns with the suffering of the Iraqi people – which was much greater in the past – or with attacking the United States and its policies?

However, rather than judging Iraq by the standards of recent international interventions, world history, or Iraqi history, the most important standard by which to judge Iraqi reconstruction is how the Iraqis themselves view the current situation. Two recent public opinion polls – one by Gallup and one by Zogby International – have provided systematic data about Iraqi views.[3] These data suggest most Iraqis are optimistic, but they do not welcome a long-term US role in Iraq. Gallup surveyed 1,178 Baghdad residents in late August and early September 2003. Asked whether the ousting of Saddam Hussein was worth any hardships they have suffered since the coalition intervention, 62% answered yes and 30% no. Among the million residents of Sadr City, the poor Shiite district of the capital, 78% of respondents answered yes, a figure that lends perspective to accounts of anti-American agitation in the area by radical Shiite Islamists (for example, firebrand cleric Muqtada Al-Sadr). In contrast, respondents from the relatively affluent mixed-sect al-Karkh district were evenly divided, with 47% answering yes and 47% no. Similar differences emerged when those polled were asked whether the Coalition Provisional Authority (CPA) is doing a good job: Sadr City respondents largely answered yes (37% positive, 13% negative), while al-Karkh respondents largely answered no (38% negative, 20% positive). The remaining respondents were neutral.

In August 2003, Zogby International polled 598 residents of Basra, Mosul, Kirkuk, and al-Ramadi, the latter a center of Sunni Arab resistance to coalition forces. The poll did not ask whether the overthrow of Saddam was worthwhile. Asked how long coalition troops should remain in Iraq, 25% of respondents answered two or more years, compared to 32% who said that coalition forces should leave in six months. The latter group included some individuals who, while friendly to the United States – for example, Ahmed Chalabi – are optimistic that Iraqis can take over within a short time.

Both these polls indicate that Iraqis are optimistic about the future. According to 67% of Baghdadis and 69% of those in the four regional cities, Iraq will be better off in five years, compared to 8% and 20%, respectively, who think the country will be worse off. When asked whether the CPA was doing a better job than it had been two months earlier, 50% of Baghdadis answered yes, only 14% said no, and 33% saw no difference. Moreover, 61% of Baghdad respondents expressed favorable views of the Iraqi Governing Council, compared to only 13% with negative views.

Although they are optimistic about improvements, Baghdadis have mixed views about the present. Asked whether Iraq is better or worse off than it was before the invasion, 29% answered "somewhat better" while 32% answered "somewhat worse," with 15% saying "much worse" and only 4% "much better" (the remaining respondents were neutral). These attitudes are no doubt related to the fact that 94% of the respondents feel that the capital is more dangerous than it was before the invasion.

One continuing problem is Iraqi suspicion toward the United States. Among Baghdadis, 44% expressed a negative view of the United States compared to only 29% offering a favorable view. In the four regional cities, 50% think the United States will hurt Iraq over the next five years while 35% think the United States will help; among Sunni Arabs in the Zogby sample, the split is 70% hurt, 13% help. (Sunni Arabs constituted roughly 27% of the Zogby sample. Although the poll results do not list Sunni Arabs separately, they do differentiate between Sunnis and Kurds; subtracting Kurds from Sunnis produces a good approximation for Sunni Arabs).

The Zogby poll also asked respondents whether Iraq should have an Islamic regime or a government that allows citizens to practice their own religion. Overall, 33% favored an Islamic government. Yet, 62% percent of Sunni Arab respondents called for an Islamic government, compared to only 27% of Shiite respondents; this finding lends perspective to reports of Shiite support for Iranian-style clerical rule.

Life in Post-Saddam Iraq:
A Mixture of Pluses and Minuses

If things are going well in Iraq by some of the relevant standards, then why the extensive reporting and analysis emphasizing the problems? Part of the reason is that the reconstruction of Iraq is being judged by the unrealistically high expectations the US government fostered during the build-up to the war. The United States hoped it could sweep aside the top political leadership while the strong technocratic bureaucracy would remain. However, these optimistic Americans underestimated the depth of Saddam's brutality and how much his terror was hiding the fact that the state had fallen apart under his misrule. When he was swept away, the reality of the state's weakness was exposed; ordinary Iraqis showed their disdain for the state with the looting. So the state has to be rebuilt, which takes time and creates problems along the way.

It was never realistic to expect that Iraq could become a prosperous, democratic, stable country within a few months. It is rather remarkable to hear complaints on this score from Middle Easterners. For instance, Arab League Secretary General Amr Musa criticized the Iraqi Governing Council, saying "forming this council through elections would have given it more force and credibility."[4] That is an extraordinary statement from the head of an organization of twenty-two countries, none of which have leaders chosen by what can be reasonably called a democratic election—Bashar Assad's election by more than 99% does not count as democratic, for instance. Indeed, the record of the Arab League states is not much to brag about in the fields of social and economic development either, as the recent *Arab Human Development Report* highlighted.[5] If Iraq only aims to match the political, economic and social performance of other Arab states, it will not be aiming very high.

To be sure, the problems rebuilding the Iraqi state have been compounded by some errors made by the Bush Administration. Planning was not adequately focused on the problems that occurred—in part because the planning centered on the pre-war expectation that there would be serious humanitarian problems like food shortages and refugee flows, which did not in fact occur. However, even with the best planning in the world, most of the problems would still have happened.

Life in post-Saddam Iraq is neither chaotic nor a disaster; rather, it is a mixture of pluses and minuses. The polling data above is fully consistent with anecdotal observations regarding the nature of post-

Saddam life in Iraq, some appearing in numerous press accounts and others gained during the author's own recent 1100-kilometer trip across southern and central Iraq riding in taxis and various beat-up cars and hitchhiking. These observations show that daily life goes on with ups and downs relative to the pre-war period.

One striking development has been the CPA's abolition of taxes. Iraq has become one huge duty-free zone, with imports flooding in at much lower prices than in the past. For example, a used Chevrolet Caprice that cost 18 million dinars ($9,000) before the war now sells for 8 million. As a result, some 300,000 imported vehicles have reportedly been sold in Iraq since the war, with mid-price used cars disappearing from the car lots of countries as far away as the United Arab Emirates. Similarly, the bazaars are full of inexpensive clothing from Southeast Asia, while the sidewalks in front of shops in Baghdad and Basra are stacked high with every type of consumer durable, especially air conditioners, freezers, washing machines and televisions. Major importers talk of excellent sales, while industrialists complain vociferously about the flood of what they claim are unfair imports, which force them to close factories—Saddam-era controls and UN sanctions created hothouse conditions for local factories, which are now facing a cold blast due to imports.

Current income levels are difficult to judge. Teachers are no doubt happy: although they have not received all of their paychecks on time, their salaries have been raised from $5–13 per month to $60 120 per month. Unemployment has risen dramatically, however, despite growth in the informal trade sector (small traders and service providers abound) and the creation of numerous CPA-funded street-sweeping and irrigation canal-cleaning crews. As for reported economic discontent among Sunni tribes, some individuals

[21]

who were close to Saddam's regime say that these tribes reacted in such a manner in the past when they did not get the large cash payoffs they demanded.

Many of the problems of the first post-war months are on their way to resolution. Gasoline stations in central urban areas had only short lines, while those in suburbs and villages had none, selling gasoline at less than 2 US cents per liter. The ubiquitous generators have made the electricity situation much better than that suggested by data on central power plant output; for $90, Iraqis can buy a quiet, 1,200-watt generator capable of running a television and numerous lights.

The key problem for Iraqi reconstruction is security. While Americans worry most about the attacks on them by the anti-coalition resistance, Iraqis have a different top priority, namely, security against thieves. From rich businessmen to taxi drivers, the primary fear in Baghdad is of being carjacked or murdered during a robbery, particularly given the fact that Saddam released all criminals from prison before his regime fell. More troops or a broader coalition would not necessarily solve this problem. Indeed, many Iraqis commented favorably on the low profile of coalition forces—the author's own 1,100-kilometer trip was interrupted by only five checkpoints, all manned by Iraqis. The Iraqi police are beginning to make their presence felt. For the first time ever, they are patrolling in cars – Saddam's police simply sat in their station houses – and Baghdad traffic officers are fitfully helping at the most clogged intersections. Outside the capital, security is vastly improved; for instance, on one Thursday night in Basra, men and women could be seen strolling in and out of the fanciest hotel with no security in sight.

The Solution for Iraq's Problems:
First, Do No Harm

In order to address the key security problem, the most important step is to put Iraqis in charge of the new government as quickly as possible. Having Iraqis in charge will do much to drain the anger of the resistance against the role of the US-led coalition.

However, how to hand over power to Iraqis is a matter that will take some skill. For instance, there is the problem of minority rights, especially how to convince Sunni Arabs that they have good prospects for the future. The best approach is to learn from experiences of democracy-building in the former Soviet bloc and in failed states in which the international community has intervened in the last decade, from East Timor to Somalia, Haiti to Bosnia, Sierra Leone to Kosovo. The most important lesson is to make haste slowly: to first create the rule of law and vigorous civil society institutions, as the building blocs of democracy. Representative institutions can best be created first on a local scale, where it is easier to hold caucuses that select local leaders and to learn the difficult skills of compromise and treating power as a responsibility rather than a license to enrich oneself—a lesson already applied in Iraq, where there are now functioning local councils in most cities and villages. Over time, national representative institutions can be created, and eventually national elections become appropriate.

Turning sovereignty over to Iraqis by March 2004, as proposed by France in the debates about a new UN Security Council resolution, would make the current problems worse. To do so would require either creating an interim government or holding quick elections. Either way, power would fall into the hands of the returned exiles, who are the only ones well enough organized to run an interim government or to win elections. The delightful paradox is that France's proposal would aid precisely those whom the Pentagon hardliners are said to have favored, such as Ahmed Chalabi.

Like the proposal to quickly hand sovereignty to Iraqis, most proposed solutions to the problems in Iraqi reconstruction would have little positive impact. In particular, the calls for more international intervention are generally unrealistic and would likely make things worse. To be sure, it would be useful to have international expertise on several technical fronts. Police training is the most urgent example: the United States does not have a national police, that responsibility being left to local and state governments, so the US government has serious problems mobilizing the personnel needed to do such training. In addition, some developing and East European countries are well placed to assist with repairing and patching Iraq's decrepit equipment, because they are more used to making such repairs and much of the old Iraqi equipment comes from the former East bloc. The US approach is by contrast more often to build anew rather than repair.

The UN has considerable expertise in political institution building, from encouraging political parties to creating voter registration rolls to writing a constitution. Other than that, however, the UN has limited resources to offer Iraq: its specialized agencies are not particularly good at economic development, and its role in providing security has been a disaster from Rwanda to Bosnia. Moreover, any UN role would come at a heavy political price, given the heavy weight in the UN system of those who opposed the Iraq war. Certainly the view among the American public is that the UN is inefficient if not ineffective. Moreover, in American eyes, the large role played in the UN by anti-democratic countries undercuts the UN's claims of legitimacy—to many Americans, the UN is typified by the election of Libya to chair a human rights group.

If the UN is an imperfect partner, Iraq's neighbors are worse. To call for an active Turkish or Iranian role in Iraq is to stir up anxieties among many Iraqis that these countries would meddle in internal Iraqi politics. In addition, most of the Arab states are not necessarily regarded as having that much to provide to the proud Iraqi people, many of whom see themselves as more educated and capable than many other Arabs. Reuel Gerecht provided a rather sharply worded evaluation of the proposal to bring in Arab troops:

> Since the dawn of the nineteenth-century, Muslim states have shown much greater confidence in the professionalism of Western soldiers than of fellow Muslims....After the first Gulf War, the Persian Gulf states made a big show of wanting the Egyptians and the Syrians, not the Americans, to assume the responsibility for their security. No Egyptian or Syrian soldier ever landed. The sheikhs and the intellectuals may hate us in their hearts; but they absolutely do not want to entrust their property, their wives, and daughters to foreign Arab Muslims.[6]

In point of fact, it is not clear that there is much need for large numbers of foreign troops or what the most appropriate technique may be to use against the continuing resistance. However, the argument can be made that large-scale operations by foreign troops have provoked resistance, especially by tribes. Indeed, checkpoints and patrols do not seem particularly popular in the Sunni Arab areas where the resistance has thrived. It may well be more appropriate to concentrate on improving intelligence and developing closer cooperation with locals, while improving mobility and quick-strike capabilities. In any case, the key security problem as perceived by Iraqis is the issue of crime, not the resistance, and soldiers are rarely effective at stopping robberies and thefts.

The one major change the Bush Administration is proposing is to inject much more cash. It is by no means clear that large amounts of aid money are appropriate. The main factor causing delays in repairing and rebuilding Iraqi infrastructure is the inevitable slowness associated with large projects, especially government-run ones. Furthermore, the delays will get worse, as the necessary transition is made to a larger Iraqi role in the major decisions, because that will require going through more discussions—gaining consensus in contemporary Iraq is cumbersome. The procedures used by aid agencies, even the best ones such as the World Bank, are slow. Any effort to short-cut the normal procedures will give rise to charges of cronyism, as the US Agency for International Development (USAID) saw when it awarded a contract for urgent work without going through the normal bidding process: critics immediately jumped on the fact that the contract was won by a company well connected with the Bush Administration. Building a large infrastructure project takes years, not months, no matter what aid agencies may claim.

Indeed, US aid funding is well in excess of what would be best for Iraq. The rule of thumb in the development field is that aid should not exceed 20% of national income, which would cap the aid going to Iraq at around $4-5 billion in 2004. The vast flood of aid being proposed by the Bush Administration seems way out of line with what the country can absorb. Comparing the aid received by Iraq with the Marshall Plan is telling. Over four years, the Marshall Plan distributed $60 billion (at today's prices), which worked out to $270 per European in the main participating countries. In just the one year 2004, the Bush Administration is proposing to provide $20 billion in aid to Iraq, or $770 for each of the 26 million Iraqis. Already, that is 2.8 times as much as the Marshall Plan on a per person basis – and the US government is saying that Iraq should receive tens of billions more in aid from other countries and international agencies. Furthermore, Washington is hinting that it may provide more funding in later years.

What makes the aid proposal for Iraq all the more problematic is that it is so out of line with the world's general record on aid. At $770 per person, the United States proposal for 2004 would put Iraq way off the scale of what other countries are receiving in aid. According to the World Bank's "World Development Indicators 2002," Palestinians received the highest per capita aid, at $214 per person; only Bosnia, at $185, was close. By comparison, the average for sub-Saharan Africa was $20; for South Asia, it was $3. Those areas are much, much poorer than Iraq. Consider a country like Ethiopia, where national income is $100 per person, of which $5 is from aid – that is $100 per year, not per week. In other words, the Bush Administration proposes to provide each Iraqi with foreign aid which is equal to the income of 7.7 Ethiopians. The cynic could suggest that if the Ethiopians caused more terrorism or threatened global political stability, they would see more dollars headed their way. However, that is not all that is at work here. Even compared to countries of great terrorism concern, the Bush Administration proposal for Iraq is in a special class. The world has become concerned about unemployed Pakistani youth educated in radical madrassas, but aid to Pakistan was a mere $7 per person, less than one percent of what the Bush Administration proposes for Iraq.

What Role for Iraq and the United States in Gulf Security?

Whatever its merits, the huge expenditure being proposed by the United States shows that it has the capacity and the will to stay the course in Iraq—something which the international community as a whole lacks. It is therefore inevitable that the United States will for years play the lead role in ensuring Iraq's security. As a practical matter of world politics, irrespective of formal treaties, the United States is now committed to the defense of Iraq, much as America was committed to the defense of Kuwait after 1990. Having dissolved the old Iraqi military, the United States has taken on the responsibility for defending Iraq from external interference until the new Iraqi forces can be fully effective, which could take many years.

It would be overly optimistic to think that the new Iraqi forces will be able to take on the full challenge of defending the country within the next few years; just taking on the full responsibility for domestic security will be a challenge. Therefore, there is likely to be an abiding US presence in Iraq, with the support of the Iraqi government. This will be entirely different in character from the current occupation. Instead, it would be more on the model of the US presence in Germany and Japan—originally begun under a US occupation but continuing as an alliance with the United States. Not many US troops would have to be stationed in Iraq in order to defend the country's borders; the model could quite possibly be how the US Air Force was hidden away in the desert of Saudi Arabia.

The abiding US presence will be a burden on US forces which they will be eager to end. Already, the United States is eager to build up Iraqi security forces as quickly as possible. America has to make sure that Iraq has domestic security forces adequate to face internal challenges, though not so large as to challenge the civilian government. To reduce the threat that a new Iraqi military may go down the same coup-making route as the old one, the United States will be reluctant to use regular military for keeping order. Thus, the

United States has started to create a series of different point-protection and paramilitary units, vaguely similar to the French gendarmes or Italian carbinieri. This process is likely to accelerate.

Iraq also has to have a conventional military capable of defending the country's borders. How quickly that can happen depends on what kind of a force is needed. The size and character of the new Iraqi forces, rebuilt with Western expertise and equipment, will depend on the threat environment in the Gulf. The United States would prefer a smaller Iraqi military, so that the Iraqi military will not threaten neighbors and will not dominate Iraqi politics. However, whether that can happen will depend on what threats Iraq faces. Iraq lives in a dangerous neighborhood. Iraq has real security problems from US friend Turkey and US foe Iran. Each would be tempted to meddle if it could. Turkey sent tens of thousands of troops into Iraq at times during the last decade, and it remains eager to wipe out the remnants of the Kurdish Worker's Party (PKK) terrorist group which are hiding in Iraq.

More generally, how far the United States goes in the rebuilding of the Iraqi military depends on the security environment in the Gulf over the next decade or more. There are two plausible scenarios. One is a scenario from which everyone would benefit, namely, a low threat environment. This should be possible now that Saddam Hussein's regime is gone. Were this to come to pass, the countries of the Gulf Cooperation Council (GCC) could put force modernizations on hold and scale back readiness, cutting back on the training and expensive exercises. Iraq could limit itself to a small border-protection force, designed more against smugglers than against a serious military threat. The United States could reduce its military presence in the Gulf to something like pre-1990 levels, and the US presence could be spread out among all the Arab states of the Gulf, without placing an undue burden on those states like Saudi Arabia which feel uncomfortable with a lasting US military presence on their soil. Were Iran willing to cooperate, it might be possible to put in place confidence- and stability-building measures, including Iraqi, US and GCC forces. That could create the atmosphere for agreements to limit the size and deployment of forces, similar to the Conventional Forces in Europe treaty.

However, it seems more likely that the Gulf is headed towards a high threat environment, because Iran looks bent on bringing to completion its nuclear weapons program. Assume for a moment that the best case occurs—Iran resolves its current difficulties with the International Atomic Energy Agency (IAEA) about Iran's non-compliance with the Treaty on the Non-Proliferation of Nuclear Weapons (NPT). Even in that case, Iran has announced plans, on which considerable progress is being made, to acquire the capability to produce substantial amounts of weapons-grade fissile material – which is permitted under the NPT for countries that fully cooperate with the IAEA. If Iran insists on proceeding with those plans, then Iran's neighbors may worry that Iran is readying itself to rapidly "break out" of NPT restrictions. To guard against that contingency, some countries might consider proliferation:

- Saudi Arabia: Worried by Iran's self-conception as the Gulf's great power and not sure the United States would protect it against Iranian intimidation, Saudi Arabia might turn to Pakistan, whose nuclear program Riyadh is thought to have financed. Were Pakistan to store on Saudi soil nuclear warheads designed to fit in the CSS-2 missiles the Saudis bought from China, that would be consistent with Saudi Arabia's obligations under the NPT, based on the precedent set by dual-key missiles the United States stored in Germany during the Cold War.

- Egypt: There is broad consensus among the Egyptian elite that great states have great armies, specifically that Egypt must have the most powerful Arab army if not the most powerful Muslim army. Indeed, faced with the perceived imbalance with Israel, Egypt has long had a strong pro-nuclear lobby. Were not only Iran but also Saudi Arabia to acquire nuclear weapons – even by the indirect Pakistani route described above – Cairo would have grave difficulties remaining non-nuclear.

- Turkey: Turkey has long been at peace with Iran, but as a militantly secular state, Turkey has to worry about a meddling Islamic Republic. While Turkey's first instinct would be to turn to NATO, it is not clear how well NATO would defend Turkey. A determined Turkey could build nuclear weapons in well under a decade.

Were Iran to have advanced nuclear capabilities which make regional states worry that it has the bomb, there is a high chance that the United States would take strong action to forestall further proliferation by other regional states—and to forestall preemptive action against Iran by Israel. That means the United States would have to increase its own presence, with more frequent military exercises and more pre-positioned equipment; Washington would have to press Arab Gulf states to permit greater access to their military bases for US soldiers. Moreover, the United States would have to provide regional states with sufficient military assets to defend themselves from this new threat. For instance, the United States might provide GCC states with more advanced anti-missile capabilities in order to counter the threat of nuclear-tipped Iranian missiles.

One implication of a nuclear-capable Iran is that America would work with Iraq to create a large, sophisticated Iraqi military. Iraq would need such a force if it were to be able to defend itself against Iranian pressure or open aggression without recourse to WMD. Furthermore, it is near inevitable that, if Iraq lacked the means to defend itself conventionally, the new Iraq would restart the Saddam-era WMD programs. To forestall that eventuality, it is quite plausible that the United States would agree to sell Iraq an impressive arsenal of weapons, including thousands of M1A1 tanks and hundreds of F-16 fighter planes. It would be most unfortunate for Iraq if its scarce funds had to be diverted to such a military build-up. One can only hope that Iran does not go down the path it has started on, namely, the path towards a regional arms race. The irony is that Iran would be guaranteed to lose any such arms race, because the Arab states of the Gulf are much richer and they have a close relationship with the world's only military superpower, the United States.

In summary, what happens to the security environment in the Gulf depends not only on how successfully Iraq stabilizes itself, but also on what path Iran takes. If Iran continues on its present announced course to acquire a wide range of nuclear capabilities, the Gulf could find itself in a new arms race, and Iraq could, with US help, become a substantial military force.

Iraq's Impact on Political Reform

While external security has been an important issue for Gulf countries, arguably as important has been internal security. There has been much debate about the impact of the Iraqi experience on the domestic security of states in the Arab world. Some have suggested that, having overthrown Saddam, the US government will now replace other Middle East governments in the name of making the region more democratic. Such a view seriously misrepresents the Bush Administration's goal in promoting political reform in the region and its hopes that Iraq can be an example for such reform.

It is not surprising that many in the Middle East are skeptical whether Washington really wants political reform in the region. Prior to September 11, 2001, promoting political liberalization was not an important US objective in the Arab world. The argument was that only friendly tyrants could make peace with Israel – witness Sadat in Egypt and Hussein in Jordan – while genuinely free elections could bring to power radical anti-Western Islamists, as was said to have happened in the 1992 Algerian elections. There was little interest in disturbing US relations with the Gulf monarchs who worked closely with America on vital issues like security and energy.

However, that has changed. In his apology after September 11, Martin Indyk described why the 1990s policy he supported was wrong:

> [It was felt that] the United States could not afford the destabilizing impact that pressure for reform would generate in deeply traditional and repressed [Arab] societies....The al Qaeda network established by bin Laden (a Saudi) and his associate Ayman al-Zawahiri (an Egyptian) wanted to overthrow the Saudi and Egyptian regimes, but with US support those had become hardened targets. So al Qaeda made a strategic decision to strike at their patron, the more powerful but also more vulnerable United States.[7]

The new policy is to promote political and economic liberalization so that discontented youth can see their problems being addressed and know they have a way to voice their complaints within the political system, which will reduce the numbers who turn to violent protest.

To accomplish this aim, political liberalization should be a gradual democratization that reinforces existing regimes rather than replacing them. Such an approach fits in well with US interests, balancing progress towards democracy with the need to preserve stability. The US government can credibly argue that expanding the scope for political participation is in the interests of undemocratic US Arab allies, even though they may pay a short-term price in the form of more openly expressed discontent when they begin to open up. For instance, faced with many socio-economic problems that can feed discontent, the Saudi regime would do well to provide a more accountable and transparent government and to provide ways to express disagreement within the framework of the political process—the alternative would be a false tranquility while radical forces gain strength in the shadows.

A long-term approach to democratization makes sense, based on the lessons of history. Democracy rarely comes in one fell swoop. The Bush Administration by no means expects the Arab world to be swept by popular revolutions overthrowing existing regimes. Democracy will not come to the Middle East post-Saddam the way it did to Eastern Europe, in a sudden wave made possible by a single transformative event—in that case, the collapse of the Soviet occupation. Much more common is a long, slow march towards democracy. Consider the US experience. The "Jeffersonian democracy" Americans are so proud of involved slave-ownership and restriction of voting to male property-owners; it took women 140 years after the Declaration of Independence to get the vote.

If Arab governments are wary that US-sponsored liberalization programs will undermine their rule, they will ensure that those programs are ineffective. To a large extent, this has been the fate of past US efforts to promote democracy in the region. To secure the cooperation of Arab governments, a program for political, social and economic reform can begin with some of the less contentious issues. While many in the Arab world may reject creating Western-style democracy, there is likely to be widespread agreement with the limited agenda of greater tolerance and personal freedom laid out in President Bush's 2002 State of the Union speech, which without mentioning democracy cited instead American support for "the rule of law; limits on the power of the state; respect for women; private property; free speech; equal justice; and religious tolerance."

To understand how slow liberalization can come to the region, consider how the winds of political reform are already beginning to stir in the region. The most interesting and important case is Saudi Arabia. In January 2003, 104 Saudis – mostly intellectuals, many quite conservative – sent Crown Prince Abdullah a "National Reform Document" calling for "more steps in building a country of constitutional institutions" such as an elected parliament, economic reform, "strengthening the internal front" with measures such as a greater role for women in society, political reforms such as greater freedom of speech, and an invitation to a "national dialogue convention." Previous, more tentative such efforts resulted in the signatories being the subject of media attacks and government harassment. By contrast, Prince Abdullah's response was to meet with 34 of the signatories and then to issue his own "Charter for Arab Reform." His aides began to remind US journalists about Abdullah's long-standing reform ideas, such as local elections and regional choice about whether women could drive. The debate about reform then picked up, with another manifesto, "In Defense of the Nation," issued in September 2003 by hundreds of prominent Saudis. It read in part:

Our country is witnessing increasing violent acts that use weapons and bloodshed as a means to prove its [sic] existence and impose its [sic] points of view instead of words and dialogue, which will generate a lot of damage on national security and social stability and civil peace...We are all invited to take our responsibility and review our steps and admit that being late in adopting radical reforms and ignoring popular participation in decision-making have been the main reasons that helped the fact that our country reached this dangerous turn, and this is why we believe that denying the natural rights of the political, cultural, and intellectual society to express its opinions has led to the dominance of a certain way of thinking that is unable to dialogue with others.[8]

These stirrings of interest in political liberalization are very interesting. How much political liberalization progresses in the Arab world in the next decade will depend much more on what happens in Iraq than on whatever else the US government does in the region. If Iraq becomes mired in instability, with petty politicians pursuing narrow interests rather than the public welfare, then the talk of democracy will look rather shallow. If Iraq makes great advances towards more representative government, that will influence the Arab world profoundly. Of course, even success in Iraq will not guarantee success for liberalization elsewhere in the Arab world. If the post-war transformation of Iraq unfolds well and a more open and representative government emerges there with strong US support, then many governments around the region will want to claim they are going with this trend, whether or not they are in fact doing so. There is a risk that political reform will follow the same path as did economic reform in the1980s and 1990s— Washington presses hard, local governments all proclaim loudly how much they are doing, and not much changes.

Conclusion:
GCC Security and Iraq's Reconstruction

The security of the entire region depends on how well the reconstruction of Iraq goes. Failure of the US-led effort in Iraq would destabilize the entire Middle East. Lebanon was a failed state in the early 1980s, it destabilized Syria, Palestine and Israel and threatened the peace of the entire region. Iraq is ten times larger than Lebanon, and it borders on six countries rather than two. If Iraq becomes a failed state, the instability would spill over into the neighboring states. Tens of thousands of Iraqis would flee, and they could create great problems, for example, Kurds fleeing into Turkey, or tribal Iraqis upsetting Jordan's delicate balance between Palestinians and East Bankers. Armed Iraqi groups would be tempted to operate in the richer lands on the other side of the border, especially in the GCC countries. When the inevitable happened and one regional state started meddling in Iraqi politics, the other regional states would do the same, each to protect its particular interests. In short, instability and problems would spread throughout the entire region.

To prevent this calamity, Gulf Arab countries have an interest in helping stabilize Iraq, and they have a humanitarian obligation to aid the Iraqi people, with whom they have deep historical and cultural links. The most obvious and elementary step would be for GCC states to agree to forgive the Saddam-era debt. It is disappointing to see oil-rich states insisting on their pound of flesh from the new Iraq, which is no more able to repay its debt than are other heavily indebted Third World countries such as Argentina which have demanded and received substantial debt reduction. The next step would be for governments in the GCC states to encourage more active interaction with Iraqis, such as scholarships for Iraqi students at Arab universities, finance for trips by Iraqi businessmen, and government-provided incentives (for example, low-cost insurance) to encourage investment in Iraq. None of these steps would require working with the US-run administration in Iraq, which might be politically difficult for some of the GCC member governments.

Deep differences remain in the international community about how best to reconstruct Iraq. At the end of the day, the decision about which approach to adopt is up to the United States, because it is the United States which took the lead in the war. For all the talk about the greater legitimacy of the United Nations, the UN is simply not willing to take charge in Iraq. The UN is unwilling to station more than a few dozen staff members in Iraq; if it is unwilling to incur risk, then the UN is in no position to take charge. Given the fact that the Americans will be the decision-makers, some governments would much rather stay away from Iraq, especially those governments that were opposed to the war in the first place. It would be unwise for those governments to base their decision about whether to get involved or stay away purely on the role the United States will play. That decision should be made by each state on the basis of its national interest. The reality is that the entire Gulf and much of the Middle East will be destabilized if Iraq fails. That would not be in the interest of any GCC state. Each GCC state has an interest in things going well in Iraq, and that should dictate their approach as to whether to become involved in the reconstruction effort.

Progress in the stabilization and reconstruction of Iraq would create a momentum for change in the Middle East that should be used to reinforce the fight against terrorism, put pressure on rogues and promote democracy. It would also free up US resources – not least of which being presidential time and attention – that could be devoted to the Arab–Israeli peace process. On the other hand, an Iraq quagmire would come to absorb more and more resources, as well as creating the image of an impotent United States. In other words, if the United States fulfills its mission in Iraq, it will not have to choose among competing priorities; if it fails in its mission in Iraq, it will not have the luxury to choose among them, either. For this reason, developments in Iraq will be the main factor determining US policy towards the Middle East in 2004—the more successful the United States is in Iraq, the more magnanimous it will be about differences with GCC states regarding the Middle East, whereas the less successful America is in Iraq, the more likely it will be to blame that failure on those who opposed the war in the first place.

2

Checking the Rising Tide:
Anti-Americanism in Iraq and the
Future of the US–Iraq Relationship

Bathsheba Crocker

Reconstructing Iraq after the 2003 war is the largest post-conflict challenge the United States (US) has undertaken since the end of World War II. It is certainly the most strategically significant. If Iraq becomes a stable, prosperous democracy, it could exert a powerful and positive influence on the region. However, if Iraq descends into chaos, the consequences would be disastrous – not only for the Iraqi people, who have suffered for more than three decades under oppressive rule – but for regional stability, America's relations with the Muslim and Arab world, and US authority in the international community as a whole.

As the early months following the war confirmed, the United States failed to prepare for peace as it had for war, or to marshal the resources to consolidate success. Given that the US role in the post-conflict reconstruction of Iraq will determine the future of US–Iraq relations, early missteps in the reconstruction efforts are particularly unfortunate.

This paper will examine several particular aspects of the US-led reconstruction efforts in Iraq that will impact on the redefinition of Iraqi nationalism and, hence, the future of US–Iraq relations, and set forth recommendations for addressing those issues so as to improve the chances of better future relations between the two countries.

Key to the nature of the future relationship will be the extent to which a redefined, post-Saddam Iraqi nationalism is premised on a strong sense of anti-Americanism, or is decidedly anti-Western. Early on in the reconstruction, it was already clear that the Iraqis' tolerance and support for an outside occupation was wearing thin. Having suffered a quick and humiliating military defeat, Iraqis' sense of nationalism then had to endure a large-scale occupation by foreign military troops. That those troops were largely American only heightened Iraqi and regional suspicion that the 2003 war in Iraq was an attempt by Washington to impose its own agenda on Iraq.[1]

The resentment of Iraqis against the United States and its occupation was further heightened by the failure of the US-led coalition to provide adequate security or instill a genuine sense of law and order in the opening months of the reconstruction. In some ways, the occupation was incredibly disruptive to Iraqi daily life – for example, coalition forces effectively closed off large sections of Baghdad to normal Iraqis – and the Iraqi people felt a decrease in their own sense of personal safety from the time of Saddam. Enduring the presence of so many foreign troops was not made easier by the sense that those troops could not protect Iraqis against common crimes, sabotage of infrastructure, guerilla warfare or terrorist attacks.

Early decisions and actions will not necessarily prejudice the possibility of a positive future relationship between Iraq and the

United States. However, seven months into the reconstruction effort, the United States was facing "make or break" time. Iraqi patience was wearing thin and the Coalition Provisional Authority's (CPA) window of opportunity for turning things around in Iraq was closing.[2]

Early on in the reconstruction efforts, US Secretary of Defense Donald Rumsfeld noted that mid-course corrections would be needed.[3] Several months later, the Bush Administration began making some corrections, returning to the United Nations (UN) for discussions on an enhanced UN role in post-war Iraq – in order to encourage other countries to increase their participation on the security and resource fronts – and submitting a supplemental budget request to Congress that would significantly increase the amount of money the United States pays for Iraq's reconstruction.

These and other attempts to turn the tide in Iraq will be critical to putting Iraq on a more promising road toward its future, and to consolidating a better relationship between Iraq and the United States. As one expert has noted, "Washington needs to ensure that the civil disorder in southern Iraq and parts of Baghdad does not develop into a large-scale anti-American protest movement or even into a revolt, as happened in 1920 following the British occupation."[4]

US–Iraq Relations

Past Relations

Relations between the United States and Iraq have been checkered over the last several decades. Throughout most of the Cold War years, Iraq's close ties to the Soviet Union led the United States to align instead with Iran and Saudi Arabia. After the 1979 revolution in Iran, however, the United States shifted its tune on Iraq, developing a policy of engagement that lasted throughout the 1980s. During that time, the United States sold arms to Iraq to support its war against Iran, and provided agricultural support and other assistance.

This policy, too, proved short-lived. After Iraq invaded Kuwait in August 1990 and Saddam Hussein failed to withdraw according to a UN imposed deadline, the United States led a coalition of military forces to drive Iraq out of Kuwait in January 1991. Despite some demands at that time to overthrow Saddam, the United States pulled its military out of Iraq before doing so, leaving Saddam in power.

The US policy again shifted after the Gulf War, turning from armed conflict to containment, a policy that was backed up by a robust package of UN economic sanctions and intrusive international weapons inspections. In addition, the United States established a "no-fly" zone over certain areas of Iraq, and the United States and the United Kingdom defended the zone with periodic aerial bombardments. Despite this internationally backed policy toward Iraq, however, Saddam became more and more able to circumvent both the sanctions regime and the weapons inspections. The UN inspection teams were ultimately withdrawn in 1998 and did not return to Iraq until the fall of 2002.

In 1991, after encouraging Iraqis to rise up in popular revolt against Saddam, the United States failed to come to the aid of Iraq's Shiites in the southern part of the country who heeded the US call. Their nascent revolution was violently quashed by Saddam's armed forces, resulting in the death of an estimated 30,000–60,000 Iraqi Shiites. Since the end of the Gulf War, the United States also covertly supported several other failed attempts to depose Saddam by coup or popular uprising. Towards the end of the 1990s, momentum began to grow in the United States in favor of an active policy of regime change. The Clinton Administration adopted regime change as US policy, and the US Congress supported the policy through the passage of the Iraq Liberation Act in 1998, which allocated $97 million in support to Iraqi opposition groups seeking the overthrow of Saddam.

It was only after the tragic events of September 11, 2001, however, that the US government began an active campaign to force Saddam from power. The Bush Administration first tried to work through the United Nations Security Council to address the issue of Iraq's weapons of mass destruction (WMD), securing the unanimous passage of Resolution 1441, which called for unconditional compliance with the long series of Security Council resolutions calling on Saddam to disarm. After a new team of UN weapons inspectors failed to find any conclusive evidence of an Iraqi WMD program and several months of increasingly contentious relations between the United States and other Security Council members, the United States eventually decided to remove Saddam by force, with the support and assistance of coalition countries.

The 2003 war was short and militarily successful – Saddam and Baghdad fell in just three weeks, on April 9, 2003 – paving the way for a new beginning for Iraq and US–Iraq relations, which for decades had been defined in the context of Saddam and his policies.

The Future of the Relationship

The road to a mutually beneficial and acceptable US–Iraq relationship will be bumpy, and will likely require compromises on both sides. The United States cannot expect to dictate the future government, political structure, or leaders of Iraq. Iraq, likewise, cannot expect the United States – having waged a war that liberated the Iraqi people from decades of oppressive rule – to merely write the checks and provide the troops necessary to reconstruct and stabilize Iraq without claiming some right to influence the future of the country.

The Bush Administration has outlined lofty goals for what a post-Saddam Iraq might look like. The President has articulated those goals to be a "decent and democratic society . . . [and] a nation of laws and free institutions."[5] He has similarly said he wants an Iraqi government that is democratic, multi-ethnic, maintains Iraq's territorial integrity, is free of WMD, and is at peace with its neighbors. Secretary Rumsfeld has talked of Iraq becoming a representative democracy, noting that, "Iraq could conceivably become a model – proof that a moderate Muslim state can succeed in the battle against extremism taking place in the Muslim world today."[6] Some Bush Administration officials have argued that the transformation of Iraq into a stable democracy could in turn transform the entire region, producing a domino effect.[7]

A moderate, democratic Iraq could obviously provide a good partner for the United States in the region. Deputy Secretary of Defense Paul Wolfowitz has noted that, like the rebuilding of Germany and Japan after World War II, a successful reconstruction of Iraq could lead to a future relationship based on friendship and peace.[8] Presumably, both Iraqis and Americans would benefit from such a relationship.

Achieving the goals the United States has laid out, however, will not be easy. The United States will have to overcome deep-seated suspicion and mistrust over its motives, contend with strong anti-American sentiment in Iraq and the region, and reverse its trend line of supporting questionably democratic rulers in the Middle East.

Moreover, certain decisions and actions by the United States in the first months of the reconstruction effort will lessen its chances of successfully redefining its relationship with Iraq.

US credibility is on the line in Iraq. How it handles the reconstruction and, in particular, whether it shows the commitment to transform its promises into reality will dictate whether Iraqis will be supportive of US efforts or become openly hostile to the US presence. This, in turn, will affect whether the United States will be successful in redefining its relationship with Iraq to one of peace and friendship.

Unfortunately, though, in the areas of security and public safety, governance and participation, the economy, basic services and oil, the United States' early record in Iraq – while positive in some respects – has helped to create a potential breeding ground for anti-Americanism in that country.

Reconstructing Post-War Iraq

Security and Public Safety

Immediately after the fall of Saddam in April 2003, Iraqis went on a massive – and unchecked – spree of looting and destruction. Government buildings, university campuses and national museums were stripped of everything from electrical wire to desks, from national antiquities to computers, from windowpanes to pencil and paper, and often burned and left completely destroyed. Coalition forces were slow to react to the looting, asserting that US forces would not engage in policing, or that the looting was merely the expression of decades of pent-up rage. Although the looting spree eventually ran its course and coalition forces began to take ownership of the public safety issue, this early experience did not leave Iraqis with the sense that the occupying forces would be able to protect them.

This uneasiness only heightened in the ensuing months. Looting gave way to organized sabotage against Iraq's fragile infrastructure – from theft of electrical copper wire to strategic attacks on water mains, power plants and oil pipelines. At the same time, criminal activity was rampant, with car jackings, rapes and ordinary theft common occurrences. Women in particular suffered—many were not able to walk freely to school or the market and could only venture outside their homes with a male relative or friend as protection. Iraqis were visibly frustrated at the lack of security, at times noting that at least under Saddam they felt safe.

At the same time, US forces came under regular attack in what became an increasingly organized guerilla insurgency campaign. By late summer 2003, terrorist activities had tragically taken root, with major bomb attacks at the Jordanian Embassy in Baghdad on August 7 (killing 17 people); the UN headquarters in Baghdad on August 19 (killing 23 people, including Sergio Vieira de Mello, the Special Representative of the Secretary-General); and the Imam Ali mosque in Najaf on August 29 (killing 90 people, including a prominent Shiite cleric Ayatollah Mohammad Baqr Al-Hakim). Resistance activities targeted Iraqis working with the coalition (such as police officers), US and international civilians and humanitarian workers, in addition to coalition troops. A series of particularly gruesome days in late October 2003 saw major bomb attacks against a hotel occupied by coalition troops and civilians working for the CPA, the International Committee of the Red Cross headquarters and several Iraqi police stations.

All of these actions were intended to undermine the efforts of the US-led coalition and test the will of the United States to stay the course despite climbing casualties among US forces. Seven months into the reconstruction efforts, the United States still lacked sufficient intelligence to determine the main source of these activities – whether former regime loyalists, ex-Baathists, a new breed of Iraqi nationalists, Islamists, or foreign fighters, perhaps with links to al Qaeda or other terrorist organizations. However, it was likely that the resistance was being driven to some extent by all of these factions and perhaps others, some working together and some ad hoc. While most Iraqis did not actively support the armed resistance or terrorist activities, there were growing signs that if the coalition does not begin to address those activities and their causes more systematically and effectively, the resistance could become organized and gain popular support.[9]

Although some of the resistance to US efforts in Iraq may not have been directly linked to US reconstruction efforts, certain early decisions and actions by the coalition are likely to have played a role in fueling anti-Americanism.

For example, the CPA's May 23, 2003 edict disbanding Iraq's armed forces left an estimated 400,000 former officers and enlisted men without jobs, feeling alienated from the coalition's efforts to secure their country, and angry at the United States, which had dropped leaflets during the war that promised protection of Iraq's military if they refrained from fighting against US forces. Laid-off former officers and soldiers may in fact be part of the anti-US insurgency in Iraq and, in some cases, may even be directing those attacks.[10] By creating a large pool of unemployed, angry and armed Iraqis, the CPA's decision may have contributed to the escalating violence in Iraq.

Although Ambassador L. Paul Bremer, the US head of the CPA, shifted course somewhat after his initial decision – deciding to pay small monthly stipends to the former military and allowing former soldiers and officers below a certain rank to be eligible to join the New Iraqi Corps (the newly formed Iraqi armed force) – dissolving the former military was seen by many as "a humiliation to the dignity of the nation."[11] Unless this humiliation is channeled into more productive energies and activities, it will continue to manifest itself as bitterness and revenge against the United States.

These feelings are heightened by what many Iraqis see as the US failure to ensure their security. After the spate of deadly bombings in August 2003, members of Iraq's Governing Council complained to Ambassador Bremer that the occupying forces were not providing adequate protection.[12] One member of the Governing Council went so far as to suspend his membership in the council, citing the "dangerous security void in Iraq" as the reason.[13] Another member of the council – the brother of Ayatollah Mohammed Baqr Al-Hakim – openly blamed coalition forces for the death of his brother, calling on US troops to leave Iraq.[14] Some Iraqi police officers that survived the bombing of their compound in Baghdad expressed anger at the United States – rather than the bombers – saying, "This is the Americans' responsibility. Iraq never had car bombings before."[15]

Turning the tide on this anger and resistance will depend in part on whether the CPA begins to entrust Iraqis with responsibility for security matters, something both Iraqis and the United States claim they are eager to do. Iraqi cabinet ministers were appointed in early September 2003 and began handling day-to-day governance matters, including internal security and policing. The coalition has been overseeing the training of a revamped Iraqi police force, an Iraqi civil defense force to protect key sites and infrastructure, and the New Iraqi Corps, although efforts on all fronts are lagging. In addition, the CPA and the Iraqi Governing Council have been discussing the formation of an Iraqi paramilitary force that would assist coalition forces' efforts to root out guerilla warfare and insurgents, and to help provide general security.[16]

All such security forces could absorb some members of Iraq's former military. Moreover, putting an Iraqi face on security tasks will be key to countering rising anti-Americanism. At the same time, however, the coalition must balance this need against the reality that coalition forces will be needed to train and oversee Iraqi forces and police officers, and handle ongoing insurgency activities, for at least several years.

A decision to create a truly multinational security force to keep the peace in Iraq could also help to shift the image away from an American occupation of Iraq. Greater international participation in the security tasks in Iraq – from peacekeepers to international civilian police – would help counter some of the resentment and resistance to the US presence and could thus protect against longer term damage to the US–Iraq relationship. In fact, on October 16, 2003, the UN Security Council passed Resolution 1511, which endorsed the creation of a multinational force, albeit under US command and control, in October 2003. Nevertheless, only a few countries stepped forward to offer significant troop reinforcements, and US troops seemed destined to remain in Iraq in large numbers at least through 2004.

Iraqis have also been angry at what some view as the lack of cultural sensitivity on the part of US troops – and in some cases by their over-zealousness in carrying out security tasks. Coalition forces' raids against mosques, use of police dogs, and searches of homes and women have greatly angered Iraqis, who see these activities as transgressions of local or religious laws. Moreover, US forces have been accused of shooting first and asking questions later, at times catching unfortunate civilians in the security crossfire. In certain cities throughout the country, US forces responded to these concerns by showing greater sensitivity to and compliance with tribal or religious customs, including by paying compensation ("blood money"), delivering formal apologies and knocking before entering private homes. Some US army and marine divisions have shown amazing restraint in the face of angry and armed mobs of people. In those areas, US forces have been able to gain or re-gain the trust of the community. Greater cultural sensitivity on the part of all coalition forces could raise the Iraqis' tolerance for the continued presence of the occupying army.

In addition to homegrown opposition to US presence in Iraq, that presence may be encouraging foreign Islamist militants – perhaps with terrorist connections – to go to Iraq to join the fight against the occupation. By September 2003, US, Iraqi and Arab officials believed that hundreds of foreign fighters, including some with links to al Qaeda, were flowing into Iraq from Syria, Iran, Saudi Arabia, Jordan and Turkey.[17] The presence of the US forces and Iraq's porous borders, chaotic security situation and general lack of political authority make it in some ways the perfect venue for militant groups.[18] "The occupation of Iraq…is a galvanizing symbol for radical Islamic groups."[19] Disgruntled former Iraqi armed services members could prove easy recruits to fundamentalist causes.

President Bush has portrayed Iraq as the "central front" in the war on terrorism, and purported links between Saddam Hussein's Iraq and terrorist activities were cited as one premise for having gone to war. Ironically, whereas before those links were tenuous at best, the war and its aftermath may be inciting a new breed of terrorism in Iraq. As one commentator remarked, "America has taken a country that was not a terrorist threat and turned it into one."[20]

If Iraq has in fact become a terrorist magnet, Iraq will continue as a central battleground in the US war on terrorism, complicating any efforts to reconfigure future US–Iraq relations on a more positive note. Anti-terrorism efforts in Iraq must continue to be a top priority for coalition forces, and every effort, both diplomatic and military, must be made to stop the flow of foreign fighters across borders.

To be truly effective in ensuring that terrorists do not take root in Iraq, however, the United States must address concerns in other areas of the reconstruction, particularly governance and the economy. Iraqis must feel a sense of ownership in the political, economic, and social transformation of their country. If not, their feelings of nationalism and opposition to the United States' efforts will only grow, as will their willingness to passively accept ongoing terrorist and resistance activities. On the other hand, if Iraq were to become a representative democracy and liberal market economy, as the US hopes, it would not be as welcome a staging ground for foreign or domestic terrorists.

Governance and Participation

How the United States manages the path toward Iraqi self-rule and sovereignty may be the most critical indicator of the future US–Iraq relationship. As Ambassador Bremer has noted, that path will be bumpy.[21] Seven months into the reconstruction effort, there were some positive signs: an Iraqi Governing Council and an Iraqi cabinet of ministers had been appointed. Local and provincial political councils had been established throughout most of Iraq. Yet, these nascent efforts were fraught with worrying pitfalls.

The Iraqi Governing Council, which was established by the CPA on July 13, 2003, is seen as lacking "the legitimacy, authority or resources to do anything about anything," in the words of one expert.[22] The Council's 25 members were handpicked by the CPA in a closed process, giving it questionable legitimacy among Iraqis, regional countries and the broader international community. Its legitimacy was also undermined by the fact that the majority of Council members were former Iraqi exiles (some with close ties to the Bush Administration) or Kurds. The Council eventually gained the grudging acceptance of the Arab League, which voted on September 10, 2003 to allow a Council member to participate in its meetings as the Iraqi representative. However, the Iraqi public remained skeptical that the Governing Council would amount to anything more than an extension of the CPA.[23]

This skepticism can be traced to the CPA's failure to articulate clearly the lines between the Council's executive authority and the CPA's own authority. Although the CPA claims that the Council can exercise real authority over policy, budgetary and other matters, most Iraqis and outsiders continue to believe that the CPA pulls the strings, because it has ultimate veto power over Council decisions. Council members themselves have stated, "[Y]ou can't blame us for anything. We don't have any responsibility."[24]

By September 2003, the international community had begun to push for more power to be devolved to the Governing Council more quickly. The US and UK-sponsored Security Council resolution that passed in October 2003 called for the Governing Council to set a timetable for drafting a constitution and holding elections; France, Germany, Russia and others called for the Governing Council to be given much greater executive authority more quickly; UN Secretary General Kofi Annan talked of forming a provisional government to which real authority would be handed. The political transformation process in Iraq must have legitimacy, in the eyes of Iraqis and the international community alike. In order to counter the perception that the United States is seeking to dominate that process, the United States should support better-defined and enhanced Governing Council powers as well as a clearly defined UN role in overseeing the political transition process in Iraq.

However, the United States essentially stuck to its own plan, calling for a linear timetable of constitution drafting, constitutional referendum and national elections before turning over full sovereignty to the Iraqis. This vision was at odds not only with what others in the international community wanted for Iraq but also with what many, if not most, Iraqis themselves wanted. The constitution drafting process was one early sign of the difficulties the United States would face in implementing its plan—members of the Governing Council could not come to agreement on how members of a constitution drafting committee should be chosen, which in turn reflected disagreement over fundamental issues, such as what role religion should play in the governance of Iraq.

The history of US engagement in the region, in addition to US behavior in the early stages of Iraq's reconstruction, has only deepened the mistrust of US motives in Iraq, supporting the argument that Washington intends to impose its own vision on Iraq rather than letting an Iraqi form of government take hold.

A true redefinition of the US–Iraq relationship will require the United States to break with its tradition in the region of supporting military rulers and monarchs who do not enjoy a popular mandate.[25] Because of this history, it has been argued that few in the Arab world – Iraqis included – are likely to believe that the US is undertaking a Wilsonian campaign to spread liberty and democracy throughout the Arab world.[26] The United States must work to gain the trust and confidence of Iraqis and people throughout the region, to show that it is serious this time in talking about democracy. Where it has in the past settled on "relationships of convenience with autocracies,"[27] the United States must now let the chips fall where they may. Any attempt by the United States to install a pro-American government or to resist majority, that is Shiite, rule in Iraq would only confirm to doubters that the United States is in fact seeking to impose its own agenda on Iraq.

Nonetheless, the United States seemed determined to play a heavy-handed – and not objective – role in directing Iraq's political process. Unfortunately, early signs pointed to a repeat of past behavioral patterns. Almost immediately after the fall of Saddam, US officials made clear what the United States would consider unacceptable in Iraq the establishment of an Iranian-style theocratic government ruled by Iraq's Shiites. Secretary Rumsfeld noted that "an Iranian-type government with a few clerics running everything in the country" was "[not] going to happen" in Iraq, vowing that "a vocal minority clamoring to transform Iraq in Iran's image will not be permitted to do so."[28] Secretary of State Colin Powell attempted to soften Rumsfeld's language, saying that Muslims would not be precluded from governing Iraq, and that it was up to the Iraqi people to decide who would govern their country.[29]

Nevertheless, the very vision that the United States has for Iraq – a Western-style democratic Iraq led by a secular pro-US government – may be directly at odds with what the majority of Iraq's population (the Shiites) would prefer. One expert has defined the Shiite vision as "an independent Iraq with a system of government that reflects their own culture and traditions and that does not serve as a base for US troops in the Persian Gulf."[30] US policy even before the 2003 war aimed at preventing radical Shiites from dominating a post-Saddam Iraq – fearing this would necessarily mean a tilt toward Iran.[31] Experts on Iraq's Shiites, though, dispute this outcome, noting that Iraq's Shiites would be loath to cede power to Tehran; that only a small minority dream of a Shiite state; and that the majority are secularists who recognize the need to work together with Iraq's other communities in order to gain the independence and freedom they all desire.[32]

Iraq's Shiites are diverse and complex. They are nationalists, having fought alongside Iraq in its war against their co-religionists in Iran in the 1980s. Although they had largely been in a wait-and-see posture toward the US-led occupation, giving the United States a grace period, by the fall of 2003 the deteriorating security situation was leading to increased anti-Americanism among the Shiite population.[33] Moreover, they "abhor the idea of an Iraqi government installed by the United States to further American interests."[34] By seeming to claim a right to dictate Iraq's future government, the United States does itself a disservice in the eyes of the majority of Iraqis. Indeed, one radical Shiite cleric in particular – Muqtada Al-Sadr – called for the establishment of a parallel Shiite government in early October 2003. Although he was not thought to command the loyalty of most Shiites, he did have a strong following, and his discontent with the US-driven political process was a worrisome sign about dissension between the Iraqi majority and the United States.

There have been other troubling signs that the United States is seeking to manipulate the future political and governance structures in Iraq. First, the makeup of the Governing Council itself reflects how the CPA – and not necessarily the Iraqi people – view Iraqi society and politics.[35] The Council is representative in the sense that its members belong to Iraq's various ethnicities and religions, and because Shiites, who make up around 60 percent of Iraq's population, dominate the Council's membership. Nevertheless, there is some concern that for the first time in Iraq's history, sectarian and ethnic identity has become the primary organizing principle in Iraqi politics.[36] Thus, the make-up of Iraq's Governing Council – which is similarly reflected in the constitutional preparatory commission and cabinet of ministers that the Council appointed – could result in the "Lebanization of Iraq," transferring power to religious and tribal leaders, weakening the country's secularists, and entrenching old rivalries.[37] One assumes that such an outcome would not make Iraq the ideal partner the United States is seeking in the region.

Second, despite having overseen the establishment of promising local and provincial political councils throughout Iraq, the CPA is tightly controlling and delaying the process of local and municipal elections, as well as the selection of candidates for such elections. The CPA argues that Iraq is not ready for free and democratic elections, and that early elections would likely benefit candidates who are hostile to the United States.[38] Although the CPA is right to be wary of rushing national-level elections, local and municipal elections would help identify and broaden the political talent base, and give ordinary Iraqis a stake in the political transformation of their country.

Shiites (and other Iraqis) perceive the delay in holding direct local and municipal elections as a means of containing their influence.[39] Moreover, Iraq's Sunnis – who make up around 20 percent of the population but who have traditionally held power in

Iraq – are worried about being dispossessed. They see US attempts to control the selection of Governing Council members or the process of local level elections as a direct threat to their rule. Such feelings of marginalization could lead Iraq's Sunnis into the arms of radical Islamists, in a "self-preservation reflex."[40] In order to show it is serious about its goal of bringing democracy to Iraq, the United States must allow local political processes to take hold, freely.

The Economy and Basic Services

Adding to Iraqis' sense of frustration with and opposition to the US presence in Iraq was the seeming inability to provide consistent vital basic services, particularly water and electricity, to the population. Most Iraqis – no friends of Saddam – seemed incredulous that a country with the might and resources of the United States could not succeed in providing basic services. Even Saddam, Iraqis argued, was able to get the electricity back up and running in just two months after the 1991 Gulf War. Some Iraqis saw the failure to provide basic services as a deliberate US ploy to control Iraq's people, or perhaps to punish them for misdeeds, as Saddam used to do.[41] By the end of a long, hot summer, Iraqis' patience with the CPA's inability to correct the power situation in Iraq was running out, and their anger about it was increasing.

Ambassador Bremer called electric power "in many ways the key to reconstruction."[42] Accordingly, in late summer 2003, the CPA ordered generators to bridge the gap between Iraq's production capacity and its electricity demand. By the fall of 2003, electricity provision throughout the country had become more regularized, although it was still far from consistent. The CPA must make every effort to ensure consistent provision of basic services to the Iraqi people, in order to stem any further erosion of support for a United States that is seen as incapable or worse.

The persistent high levels of unemployment in Iraq – estimates range up to 60 percent – similarly fueled opposition to the US efforts. Discussions among US government officials about the wisdom of privatization versus revival of state-owned enterprises largely blocked the restarting of the economy. In addition to having dismissed the 400,000 or so members of Iraq's former military and tens of thousands of former Baath party members, in line with the CPA's de-Baathification order, the majority of employees of Iraq's state-owned enterprises – numbering between 400,000 to 750,000 – remained out of work many months into the reconstruction efforts, and most state-owned enterprises remained closed.[43]

Initially, US government officials planned sweeping reforms of Iraq's controlled, socialist economy, calling for the privatization of state-owned enterprises, a stock market and fundamental tax reform.[44] They planned to establish a market economy "based on clear property rights, on a sound rule of law, [and] on economic freedom."[45]

The CPA eventually began to involve the Iraqi Governing Council in discussions surrounding the issues of privatization and foreign investment. At the CPA's urging, the Governing Council announced a series of sweeping changes to Iraq's laws that will allow foreign investment, privatization and foreign ownership of property—all radical changes in a country traditionally resistant to outside ownership of property. While perhaps wise long-term goals, it is worrisome that such changes are being imposed by two unaccountable political bodies – the CPA and the Governing Council.

Without a social safety net in place, moreover, such moves could mean continuing unemployment on a large scale, which will only feed into any growing resistance or organized opposition to the US presence in Iraq. A major US-led effort to provide jobs and to get salvageable state-owned enterprises up and running in the short-term would help stem this tide, in addition to tapping into Iraq's most valuable resource—its talented and capable people. The United States did not appear to be pursuing such plans, however, and the continuing "economic paralysis" will only serve to increase Iraqi hostility to the occupying forces.[46]

There is one economic issue on which US behavior to date could benefit the future US-Iraq relationship—Iraq's debt. Estimates for the debt itself range from $60 billion to $130 billion dollars; reparations claims related to the Gulf War add over $200 billion to that number.[47] Without some combination of a moratorium on paybacks, massive debt restructuring and a significant degree of debt forgiveness, paying back its international obligations would cripple any attempt to restart Iraq's economy.

The United States has argued consistently for debt forgiveness or at least relief. Other creditor countries – notably France, Germany and Russia, who are owed significant amounts in payments for loans made to Saddam's regime – have argued instead for debt rescheduling, without write-offs or forgiveness.[48] The United States would be well served to push the international creditor community – publicly – to handle the debt issue in a manner that is most fair to the Iraqi people and that gives Iraq the best chance to recover. In addition to being necessary, given the myriad demands on Iraq's limited revenues, such a position might be taken as a sign of goodwill by the Iraqi people.

Rebuilding a functioning Iraqi economy and transforming it into the liberal, market economy US officials would like to see will be a daunting and long-term challenge. If successful, it would result in a better trading partner for the United States in the region, and more stable investment and business opportunities for US companies. Iraqis too would presumably benefit from a more open and productive economic relationship with the United States. Nevertheless, it will be crucial that the CPA be seen to leave long-term economic decisions to the Iraqis themselves so that the United States is not seen as imposing its own vision for the future. It will be equally crucial for the United States to address Iraqis' resentment over the lack of jobs in particular, which led to angry, anti-American protests through the streets of Baghdad in the fall of 2003.

Iraq's Oil

The United States faces perhaps its biggest hurdle in persuading the Iraqi people and Iraq's neighbors that it has only benign intentions with respect to Iraq's oil. So-called "oil nationalism" has been a consistent theme among Iraqis (both supporters and opponents of Saddam Hussein) since the end of the 1991 Gulf War.[49] Both before and after the fall of Saddam in 2003, the Bush Administration insisted that Iraq's oil wealth will be used for the benefit of the Iraqi people. Security Council Resolution 1483, passed on May 22, 2003, sets forth that all Iraqi oil sales shall be audited by an international advisory and monitoring board, and that all proceeds from sales shall be deposited in a Development Fund for Iraq that is to be dispersed – at the discretion of the CPA in consultation with the interim Iraqi authority – for humanitarian and reconstruction purposes benefiting the Iraqi people.[50]

[62]

Yet, in spite of, or perhaps because of, such pronouncements, Iraqis remained deeply skeptical of US intentions with respect to their oil, seeing early shipments of oil as proof that the United States intended to steal Iraq's natural patrimony. The US decision to limit all initial contracts involving reconstruction of the oil sector to US companies fueled these concerns. Resolution 1483's call for an international oil advisory and monitoring board – which was to be chaired by a US oil company executive – seemed only to confirm suspicion that the US and its allies had gone to war to secure access to Iraq's oil and privatize its state-run oil companies.[51]

After several months of failed attempts to create the international board, the United States abandoned the effort in late August 2003, deciding instead to let Iraq's highly capable oil technocrats and Governing Council determine the future course of the industry, including the highly sensitive issue of whether to privatize Iraq's oil sector. In doing so, the United States gave up some measure of control over decisions about Iraq's oil industry, which will be critical to how much oil revenue is available to offset soaring reconstruction costs.

The decision to scrap the advisory board was largely driven by resistance among Iraq's oil sector and reluctance on the part of international oil executives to sit on the board. However, the move – which will put Iraqis more firmly in the driver's seat in making decisions about the oil industry – could also go some way toward thwarting active resistance to restarting and increasing oil production. The Iraqi campaign of sabotage against key infrastructure included attacks against crucial oil pipelines, disrupting the flow of oil for export in the early reconstruction months. Insurgents have vowed to do whatever they can to block production and exports of oil.[52]

In order to protect itself against continuing mistrust about and active resistance to its goal of revitalizing Iraq's oil industry, the United States must ensure that all decisions regarding levels of production, handling of revenues, exports and the future of the industry are made in a completely transparent and above board manner. The lack of an international advisory and monitoring board should not preclude transparent, public decision-making.

Moreover, the United States should back the creation of mechanisms by which the Iraqi people can begin to benefit from their oil bounty. Various ideas have been floated, including the establishment of a trust fund, like that in Alaska, that would distribute shares in oil wealth to all Iraqis on an annual basis. Proponents of such a plan highlight its dual benefits—it would help counter the belief that Americans want to keep Iraq's oil wealth for themselves, and it would give Iraqis a more direct stake in the future success of their country.[53]

Regardless of any ultimate decision on what such a mechanism should look like, future US–Iraq relations would benefit from a concerted US effort to show that it does not intend to exploit and embezzle Iraq's oil. Otherwise, oil nationalism – like every form of Iraqi nationalism – will become more and more focused on anti-Americanism, and spoilers will continue to make every effort to destroy Iraq's oil industry, seeing that industry as more beneficial to the United States than to Iraqis themselves.

Conclusion

Ensuring a more positive US–Iraq relationship in the future will require the United States to walk a fine line. The United States must take ultimate responsibility for a successful reconstruction—from providing for the public safety and enabling a transition to Iraqi self-rule to reestablishing basic services and revitalizing Iraq's economy. At the same time, the United States must avoid being too heavy-handed and dictating Iraq's future. The United States must not be seen to predetermine whether Iraq should be a Western-style democracy, cannot expect to handpick who can be elected, and should not force sensitive economic decisions such as whether to privatize Iraq's state-owned enterprises.

Based on US history and reputation (perhaps particularly in Iraq and the region), this may be a tough sell. The United States typically favors democracy in the Middle East so long as the "democratic" process produces leaders acceptable to Western interests.[54] There have been some worrying signs that the United States might be heading down this familiar road in Iraq. Doing so would be disastrous to the future of the US–Iraq relationship if it provoked a nationalist backlash to US efforts in Iraq. As one expert has noted, "ousting Saddam Hussein has not earned for [the United States] the privilege of dominating Iraq for the indefinite future."[55]

The United States would be wise to recognize this. Certain decisions and actions by the CPA in the early months of the reconstruction have seemed to do so. Thus, the CPA seems to have decided to leave long-term oil-related decisions to the Iraqis themselves.

The United States must redouble its efforts, provide sufficient resources and show long-term commitment. Moreover, and perhaps more importantly, the United States must demonstrate a willingness to cede authority to Iraqis and to the broader international community. Otherwise it will continue to feed the rumor mills of those who see US efforts in Iraq as merely one more example of the US campaign to spread its own agenda in the region.

The United States must overcome deeply entrenched mistrust and suspicion of its motives in order to prove to Iraqis that it is acting in good faith. If it fails to do so, a strong anti-Americanism could take root in Iraq, dooming the countries' future relations.

FUTURE OUTLOOK

Political Scenarios
in Post-War Iraq

Kenneth Katzman

Five months after the fall of the Baathist regime of Saddam Hussein, United States (US) policy toward Iraq was in major difficulty. There had been a belief in the Bush Administration that overthrowing Saddam Hussein by using direct US military force would be a panacea for Iraq and the region. However, US policy in Iraq after the US military overthrow of Saddam Hussein has encountered significant obstacles. The Iraqi people have been liberated from Saddam Hussein's brutality, but no true Iraqi government has yet replaced him, and the United States remains in effective charge of Iraq. The Iraqi people are frustrated at the slow pace of reconstruction, and resistance is growing in intensity and scope.

The Development of the Opposition to Saddam

A key to understanding the contending factions in post-Saddam Iraq is to examine the relationship between these factions, primarily exiles, and the United States in the aftermath of the 1991 Gulf War. Many of the groups, movements and parties that the United States has backed against Saddam Hussein since 1991 are major players in post-Saddam Iraq today.

Prior to the launching on January 16, 1991 of Operation Desert Storm, an operation that reversed Iraq's August 1990 invasion of Kuwait, President George H.W. Bush called on the Iraqi people to overthrow Saddam. Within days of the end of the Gulf War, on February 28, 1991, Shiite Muslims in southern Iraq, primarily Islamist in ideology, and Kurdish factions in northern Iraq launched significant rebellions. They were emboldened by the regime's defeat and the hope of US support. The revolt in southern Iraq reached the suburbs of Baghdad, but the Republican Guard forces had survived the war largely intact – having been withdrawn from battle prior to the US ground offensive – and they defeated the Shiite rebels by mid-March 1991. Kurds, benefiting from a US-led "no-fly zone" established in April 1991, drove Iraqi troops out of much of northern Iraq and subsequently remained largely free of Baghdad's rule.

According to press reports, the Administration of President George H.W. Bush believed that a coup by elements within the current regime could produce a favorable new government without fragmenting Iraq. Many observers, however, including neighboring governments, feared that Shiite and Kurdish groups, if they ousted Saddam, would divide Iraq into warring ethnic and tribal factions, opening Iraq to influence from neighboring Iran, Turkey and Syria.

Reports in July 1992 of a serious but unsuccessful coup attempt suggested that the US strategy might ultimately succeed. However, there was disappointment within the George H.W. Bush Administration that the coup had failed, and a decision was made to shift the US approach from promotion of a coup to supporting insurgency by the diverse opposition groups that had led the post-war rebellions. At the same time, the Kurdish, Shiite and other opposition elements were coalescing into a broad and diverse movement that appeared to be gaining support internationally. This opposition coalition was seen as providing a vehicle for the United States to build a viable overthrow strategy.

The First Opposition Coalition

The Iraqi National Congress

The growing opposition coalition took shape in an organization called the Iraqi National Congress (INC). The INC was formally constituted when the two main Kurdish militias – the Kurdistan Democratic Party (KDP) and the Patriotic Union of Kurdistan (PUK) – participated in a June 1992 meeting of dozens of opposition groups in Vienna. In October 1992, major Shiite Islamist groups came into the coalition when the INC met in Kurdish-controlled northern Iraq.

The INC appeared viable because it brought under one banner varying Iraqi ethnic groups and diverse political ideologies, including nationalists, ex-military officers and defectors from Iraq's ruling Baath Party. The Kurds provided the INC with a source of armed force and a presence on Iraqi territory. Its constituent groups publicly united around a platform that appeared to match US values and interests, including human rights, democracy, pluralism, "federalism" (see below), the preservation of Iraq's territorial integrity and compliance with United Nations Security Council (UNSC) resolutions on Iraq.[1] However, many observers doubted the INC's commitment to democracy, because most of its groups have

[71]

an authoritarian internal structure and because of inherent tensions among its varied ethnic groups and ideologies. The INC's first Executive Committee consisted of KDP leader Masud Barzani, ex-Baath Party and military official Hassan Naqib, and moderate Shiite cleric Mohammad Bahr Al-Ulum. (Barzani and Bahr Al-Ulum are now on the 25-member post-war Governing Council, inaugurated on July 13, 2003, and both are part of its nine member rotating presidency.)

Ahmad Chalabi

When the INC was formed, its Executive Committee selected Ahmad Chalabi, who is about 58 years old, a secular Shiite Muslim from a prominent banking family, to run the INC on a daily basis. Chalabi was educated at Massachusetts Institute of Technology (MIT) in the United States, as a mathematician. He fled Iraq to Jordan in 1958, when the Hashemite monarchy was overthrown in a military coup. This coup occurred 10 years before the Baath Party took power in Iraq (July 1968). In 1978, he founded the Petra Bank in Jordan but later ran afoul of Jordanian authorities on charges of financial malfeasance (embezzlement) and he left Jordan in 1989. In 1992, he was convicted in absentia of embezzling $70 million from the bank and sentenced to 22 years in prison. The Jordanian government subsequently repaid depositors a total of $400 million. Chalabi maintains that the Jordanian government was pressured by Iraq to turn against him, and he asserts that he has since rebuilt ties to the Jordanian government. Yet, in April 2003, senior Jordanian officials, including King Abdullah, called Chalabi "divisive" and stopped just short of saying he would be unacceptable to Jordan as leader of Iraq. Chalabi's critics acknowledge that, despite allegations about his methods, he has been single-minded in his determination to overthrow Saddam Hussein, and he is said to be the favorite of those Administration officials, particularly in the Department of Defense, that were the most supportive of changing Iraq's regime by force.

Since Chalabi returned to Iraq, there have been no large public demonstrations supportive of him or the INC, indicating that he does not have a large following inside Iraq. His most important support base appears to be the US Administration and its forces and civilian personnel in Iraq, rather than the Iraqi public. However, anecdotal press reporting suggests that he has attracted some support from those Iraqis that most welcomed the US military offensive against Saddam and subsequent occupation of Iraq.

Chalabi is part of a grouping of five major party leaders – later expanded to seven – that began meeting among themselves, prior to the 2003 war, in the hope of forming a transition government after Saddam was removed. The parties in the grouping are represented on the Governing Council. Chalabi is a member of the Governing Council and one of the nine that will rotate its presidency. He was chairman during the month of September 2003.

The Kurds: KDP and PUK

The Kurds, probably the most pro-US of all the groups in Iraq, do not have ambitions to play a major role in governing Arab Iraq, but Iraq's neighbors have always been fearful that the Kurds might still seek outright independence. In the post-Saddam period, the Kurds are participating directly in governance bodies in Baghdad. For example, longtime KDP foreign policy chief Hoshyar Zebari is Iraq's new Foreign Minister.

The major Kurdish parties were original members of the INC. In committing to the concept of federalism, the INC platform assured the Kurds substantial autonomy within a post-Saddam Iraq. Iraq's

Kurds have been fighting intermittently for autonomy since their region was incorporated into the newly formed Iraqi state after World War I. Iraq became an independent kingdom in 1932, although it remained under British influence until the 1958 fall of the British-installed monarchy. In 1961, the KDP, then led by founder Mullah Mustafa Barzani, current KDP leader Masud Barzani's father, began an insurgency that continued until the US-led protected zone was set up after the 1991 Gulf War. The Kurdish insurgency was interrupted by periods of autonomy negotiations with Baghdad. Together, the PUK and KDP have about 40,000–60,000 fighters, some of which are trained in conventional military tactics. Both Barzani and PUK leader Jalal Talabani were part of the major party grouping that has now been incorporated into the Governing Council and both are part of the Council's rotating presidency.

Radical Islamist Kurds, Ansar al-Islam and Al Qaeda

In the mid-1990s, the two main Kurdish parties enjoyed good relations with a small Kurdish Islamic faction, the Islamic Movement of Iraqi Kurdistan (IMIK), which is headed by Sheikh Ali Abdul Aziz. Based in Halabja, Iraq, the IMIK publicized the effects of Baghdad's March 16, 1988 chemical attack on that city and it allied with the PUK in 1998.

A radical faction of the IMIK split off in 1998, calling itself the Jund al-Islam (Army of Islam). It later changed its name to Ansar al-Islam (Partisans of Islam). This faction was led by Mullah Krekar, who was detained in Europe in August 2002 and now lives in Norway. Mullah Krekar reportedly studied under Sheikh Abdullah Al-Azzam, an Islamic theologian of Palestinian origin who was the spiritual mentor of Osama bin Laden. Ansar al-Islam reportedly associated itself with al Qaeda and hosted in its northern

[74]

Iraq enclave al Qaeda fighters who had fled the 2001 US-led war in Afghanistan. Prior to Operation Iraqi Freedom, during which its base was captured, there were about 600 fighters in the Ansar al-Islam enclave, located near the town of Khurmal.[2] Ansar fighters clashed with the PUK around Halabja in December 2002, and Ansar gunmen were allegedly responsible for an assassination attempt against PUK Prime Minister Barham Salih in April 2002.

The leader of the Arab contingent within Ansar al-Islam is said by US officials to be Abu Musab Zarqawi, an Arab of Jordanian origin who reputedly fought in Afghanistan. Zarqawi has been linked to al Qaeda plots in Jordan during the December 1999 millennium celebration, the assassination in Jordan of US diplomat Lawrence Foley in 2002, and to reported attempts also in 2002 to spread the biological agent ricin in London and possibly other places in Europe. In a presentation to the UNSC on February 5, 2003, Secretary of State Powell tied Zarqawi and Ansar to Saddam Hussein's regime, which might have viewed Ansar al-Islam as a means of pressuring Baghdad's Kurdish opponents. Although Zarqawi reportedly received medical treatment in Baghdad in May 2002 after fleeing Afghanistan, many experts believed Baghdad–Ansar links were tenuous or even non-existent. Baghdad did not control northern Iraq even before Operation Iraqi Freedom.[3] Zarqawi's current whereabouts are unknown, although some unconfirmed press reports indicate he might have fled to Iran after the fall of the Ansar camp to US-led forces. Some press accounts since July 2003 have said that Iran might have him in custody. US officials said in August 2003 that some Ansar fighters might have remained in or re-entered Iraq and are participating in the resistance to the US occupation, possibly including organizing acts of terrorism such as the August 19 bombing of the UN headquarters in Baghdad.

Shiite Islamist Organizations

Post-war Iraqi governance is likely to hinge on the outcome of power struggles within the Shiite Islamist community in Iraq. No other groupings have yet shown the strength to mobilize large numbers of Iraqis in the streets, as have the Shiite Islamist groupings. The Shiite Islamist groups have a well-defined structure and the ability to communicate with and organize their followers. They control individual militias, as do the Kurds. The United States sought to work with some Shiite Islamist opposition factions during the 1990s, but the US relationships with these groups was marked by suspicion, primarily because of the relationship of the Shiite Islamist groups to Iran. However, the United States has recognized the vital role these organizations are likely to play in stabilizing post-war Iraq and Shiite Islamist factions hold at least five seats on the Governing Council unveiled on July 13, 2003.

SCIRI/Badr Brigades

The most well known among the Shiite Islamist groups is the Supreme Council for the Islamic Revolution in Iraq (SCIRI), which was a member of the INC in the early and mid-1990s but progressively distanced itself from the INC banner. SCIRI was set up in 1982 to increase Iranian control over Shiite opposition groups in Iraq and the Arabian Gulf states. SCIRI's leader, Ayatollah Mohammed Baqr Al-Hakim, was the late Ayatollah Khomeini's choice to head an Islamic Republic of Iraq, a vision that, if realized, might conflict with US plans to forge a democratic Iraq. Baqr Al-Hakim and his family fled Iraq to Iran in 1980, during a major crackdown on Shiite activist groups by Saddam Hussein. Saddam feared that Iraqi Shiite Islamists, inspired and emboldened by the Islamic revolution in Iran in 1979, posed a major threat to his regime. Prior to the formation of SCIRI, Al-Hakim and his family were leaders of the Da'wa (Islamic Call) Party (see below). Ayatollah Mohammed Baqr Al-Hakim is the son of the late Ayatollah Muhsin Al-Hakim, who was a prominent Shiite leader in southern Iraq and an associate of Ayatollah Khomeini when Khomeini was in exile in southern Iraq from 1964 to 1978. He returned to Iraq on May 10, 2003, welcomed by crowds in Basra and Najaf, but he was killed in an August 29, 2003 car bombing of the mosque of Ali in Najaf. His younger brother, Abdul Aziz, now heads SCIRI.

In addition to its agents and activists in the Shiite areas of Iraq, SCIRI has about 10,000–15,000 fighters/activists organized into "Badr Brigades" (named after a major battle in early Islam) that, during the 1980s and 1990s, conducted forays from Iran into southern Iraq to attack Baath Party officials there. The Badr Brigades have long been headed by Abdul Aziz, who returned to Iraq on April 20, 2003, to pave the way for Mohammed Baqr's return. (Another Al-Hakim brother, Mahdi, was killed in Sudan in May 1990, allegedly by agents of Iraq's security services.) Iran's Revolutionary Guard, which is politically aligned with Iran's hard line civilian officials, has been the key patron of the Badr Brigades, providing them with weapons, funds and other assistance. The Badr Brigades fought alongside the Guard against Iraqi forces during the Iran–Iraq war. Many Iraqi Shiites view SCIRI as an Iranian creation and SCIRI/Badr Brigades operations in southern Iraq prior to Operation Iraqi Freedom did not spark broad popular unrest against the Iraqi regime. Some Badr fighters deployed inside northern Iraq on the eve of Operation Iraqi Freedom, and the rest have since entered Iraq.

The Badr Brigades deployed throughout Najaf in the aftermath of the August 29, 2003 bombing there that killed Al-Hakim, in what may foreshadow the formation of individual and ethnically-based militias. If each community in Iraq believes that the United States cannot provide security, then they will form their own militias and it will be difficult to build a true national army and sense of Iraqi nationhood. This already appears to be happening.

A variety of press reports say that individual militias now providing security in many towns in southern Iraq are linked to the Badr Brigades. One such militia is derived from the fighters who challenged Saddam Hussein's forces in the marsh areas of southern Iraq, around the town of Amara, north of Basra. It goes by the name Hizbollah (Party of God)-Amara, and it is headed by marsh guerrilla leader Abdul Karim Mohammedawi, nicknamed "Prince of the Marshes," who was named to the Governing Council. He is widely perceived as an ally of SCIRI.

Until August 2002 when Abdul Aziz Al-Hakim joined other opposition figures for meetings in Washington, DC, SCIRI had publicly refused to work openly with the United States or accept US assistance, although it was part of the INC and did have contacts with the United States prior to the 2003 war effort. Since the fall of the regime on April 9, SCIRI leaders have criticized what they called an illegitimate US occupation of Iraq and have called for the rapid establishment of an Iraqi self-rule authority, while at the same time publicly opposing the use of violence against the occupation. Even though Ayatollah Mohammed Baqr Al-Hakim said, upon returning to Iraq after the fall of Saddam, that he was for a democracy and would not seek to establish an Iranian-style Islamic republic, US officials are said to be mistrustful of SCIRI and have been seeking to disarm its fighters. Suggesting that SCIRI saw its interests in a degree of cooperation with the occupation, Abdul Aziz Al-Hakim did meet with other opposition leaders in late April

2003 at a post-war governance planning session sponsored by US officials. He later helped constitute the major party core of the Governing Council, and Abdul Aziz is part of the nine-person rotating Council presidency. Unlike some other Shiite Islamist groups, SCIRI has had good working relations with some Sunni oppositionists and the Kurds.

Da'wa Party

The Da'wa Party, Iraq's oldest formal Shiite Islamist grouping, continues to exist as a separate group, but many Da'wa activists appear to be at least loosely allied with SCIRI. Da'wa is a factor in post-war Iraq insofar as it is aligned with SCIRI. The party was founded in 1957 by a revered Iraqi Shiite cleric, Ayatollah Mohammed Baqr Al-Sadr, a like-minded associate of Ayatollah Khomeini. Baqr Al-Sadr was hung by the Iraqi regime in 1980 for the Da'wa's alleged responsibility in fomenting Shiite anti-regime unrest following Iran's 1979 Islamic revolution. That unrest included an attempted assassination of senior Iraqi leader Tariq Aziz. Da'wa was part of the major party council grouping that is now in the Governing Council. Da'wa's spokesman, Ibrahim Jafari, and its leader in Basra, Abdal Zahra Othman, are on the Council, as is a former Da'wa activist turned London-based human rights activist, Muwaffaq Al-Ruba'i. Jafari is one of the nine members of the Council that is rotating the presidency, and Jafari was the first to take that post for August 2003.

The Kuwaiti branch of the Da'wa Party was allegedly responsible for a May 1985 attempted assassination of the Amir of Kuwait and the December 1983 attacks on the US and French embassies in Kuwait. The Hizbollah organization in Lebanon was founded by Lebanese clerics loyal to Ayatollah Baqr Al-Sadr and the late Ayatollah Khomeini, and there continue to be some

[79]

personal and ideological linkages between Hizbollah and the Da'wa Party. The Hizbollah activists who held US hostages in that country during the 1980s often linked release of the Americans to the release of 17 Da'wa Party prisoners held by Kuwait for those offenses. Some Iraqi Da'wa members look to Lebanon's senior Shiite cleric Sheikh Mohammed Hossein Fadlallah, who was a student and protégé of Ayatollah Mohammed Baqr Al-Sadr, for spiritual guidance.

Sadr Movement: Muqtada Al-Sadr

Members of the clan of the late Ayatollah Mohammed Baqr Al-Sadr have become highly active in post-Saddam Iraq. The Sadr clan, based in Iraq during Saddam Hussein's rule, was repressed and not politically active during that time. The United States had no contact with this grouping prior to the 2003 war and did not attempt to enlist it in any overthrow efforts during 1991–2002. Although the Al-Sadr clan has been closely identified with the Da'wa Party, it appears that members of the clan and their followers currently are operating in post-war Iraq as a grouping separate from the Da'wa.

Another revered member of the clan, Mohammed Sadiq Al-Sadr, and two of his sons were killed by Saddam's security forces in 1999. A surviving son, Muqtada Al-Sadr, who is about 27 years old, has attempted to rally his followers to attain a prominent role in post-Saddam Shiite politics. He and his clan apparently have a large following in the poorer Shiite neighborhoods of Baghdad, which, after the fall of the regime on April 9, renamed their district "Sadr City," from the former name of "Saddam City." His movement also seems to attract younger followers than does SCIRI. However, Muqtada is viewed by Iran and many Iraqi Shiites as a young radical who lacks religious and political weight.

Muqtada's reputation may have been tarnished in early April when Muqtada Al-Sadr reportedly killed Abdul Majid Al-Khoei, the son of the late Grand Ayatollah Abdul Qasem Musavi Al-Khoei, shortly after his return to Najaf from exile in London. Abdul Majid Al-Khoei headed the Khoei Foundation, based in London, and he returned to Iraq after US-led forces took Najaf. Grand Ayatollah Al-Khoei differed with the political doctrines of Ayatollah Khomeini of Iran.

The Sadr grouping has not been included in the Governing Council. Muqtada has used his Friday prayer sermons in Kufa and other forums to denounce the Council as a puppet of the US occupation. In July 2003, Muqtada and his aides began recruiting for an Islamic army, for now unarmed, that Al-Sadr says must challenge the US occupation with force. He is also openly calling for a cleric-led Islamic state similar to that of Iran.

Ayatollah Al-Sistani: Hawza al-Ilmiyah

The revered Grand Ayatollah Ali Al-Sistani, based in Najaf, was repressed during Saddam's rule but is emerging as a major potential force in post-war Iraq. Perhaps the more so following the passing of Ayatollah Al-Hakim of SCIRI, although the Sadr movement will likely also benefit politically from that event. The United States had no contact with Al-Sistani when Saddam was in power. He is the most senior of the four Shiite clerics that lead the Najaf-based "Hawza al-Ilmiyah," a major grouping of seminaries and Shiite clerics. The Hawza, which is well funded through donations, is becoming an important source of political authority in the Shiite regions of Iraq. Al-Sistani himself, now free of a long house arrest imposed by Baghdad, has a large following of former students throughout the Shiite portions of Iraq. Al-Sistani and the Hawza are generally allied with SCIRI in the intra-Shiite power struggle, seeking to contain Muqtada Al-Sadr, who Al-Sistani and SCIRI both view as radical and impulsive. Al-Sistani, who is of Iranian origin, is considered to be in the tradition of Ayatollah Al-Khoei in opposing a direct role for clerics in governmental affairs, and Al-Sistani and the Hawza have spoken against a direct role for the clerics in governing post-war Iraq. However, in early July 2003, Al-Sistani began to take a more active role in Iraq's post-war decision-making by issuing a statement that only elected Iraqis – not a US-appointed governing council – should draft a constitution.

Islamic Amal

SCIRI has been allied with another Shiite Islamist organization called the Islamic Amal (Action) Organization. In the early 1980s, Islamic Amal was under the SCIRI umbrella but later broke with it. It is headed by Mohammed Taqi Modarassi, who returned to Iraq from exile in Iran in April 2003, after Saddam Hussein's regime fell. Islamic Amal, which has a following among Shiite Islamists mainly in Karbala, conducted attacks against Saddam Hussein's regime in the 1980s. However, it does not appear to have a following nearly as large as SCIRI or the other Shiite Islamist groups. Modarassi's brother, Abdul Hadi, headed the Islamic Front for the Liberation of Bahrain, which tried to stir up Shiite unrest against the Bahrain regime in the 1980s and 1990s (see below). Since returning to Iraq in April 2003, Mohammed Taqi has argued against violent opposition to the US occupation, saying that such a challenge would plunge Iraq into civil warfare.

Schisms Among Anti-Saddam Groups

In the mid-1990s, the differences among the various anti-Saddam organizations led to the near collapse of US efforts to change Iraq's regime. In May 1994, the KDP and the PUK began clashing with each other over territory, customs revenues and other issues. The PUK lined up support from Iran while the KDP sought and received countervailing backing from its erstwhile nemesis, the Baghdad government. In late August 1996, the KDP asked Baghdad to provide armed support for its capture of Irbil from the rival PUK. Iraq took advantage of the request to strike against the INC base in Salahuddin, a city in northern Iraq.

The Iraqi National Accord

The infighting in the opposition in the mid-1990s caused the United States to briefly revisit the "coup strategy" by renewing ties to a non-INC group, the Iraq National Accord (INA).[4] The INA, originally founded in 1990 with Saudi support, consists of military and security defectors who were perceived as having ties to disgruntled officials currently serving within their former organizations. It is headed by Dr. Iyad Al-Alawi, former president of the Iraqi Student Union in Europe and a physician by training. He is a secular Shiite Muslim, but most of the members of the INA are Sunni Muslims. The INA's prospects appeared to brighten in August 1995 when Saddam's son-in-law Hussein Kamil Al-Majid – architect of Iraq's weapons of mass destruction programs – defected to Jordan, suggesting that Saddam's grip on the military and security services was weakening. Jordan's King Hussein agreed to allow the INA to operate from there. The INA was ultimately penetrated by Iraq's intelligence services and, in June 1996, Baghdad dealt it a serious setback by arresting or executing INA sympathizers in the military.

Prior to Operation Iraqi Freedom, Al-Alawi claimed that the INA continued to operate throughout Iraq, and it had apparently rebuilt itself to some extent since the June 1996 arrests. However, it does not appear to have a large following in Iraq. Al-Alawi was part of the major party grouping that became the core of the Governing Council and has been named a member of that Council and one of its nine-member rotating presidency.

An INA member, Nuri Badran, has been named Interior Minister in the new cabinet, sworn in on September 3, 2003. He is attempting to build on the INA's contacts among ex-Baathists and ex-military people to develop a new domestic intelligence network, although recruitment of such categories of Iraqis might raise suspicions from other Governing Council members, such as Ahmad Chalabi. Chalabi has been the most vocal of all major post-Saddam figures in calling for the complete dismissal and isolation of all those with ties to the former regime.

Attempting to Rebound from 1996 Setbacks

For the two years following the anti-Saddam opposition groups' 1996 setbacks, the Clinton Administration had little contact with these groups. In those two years, the INC, INA and other opposition groups attempted to rebuild their organizations and their ties to each other, although with mixed success.

Iraq Liberation Act

Iraq's obstructions of UN weapons of mass destruction (WMD) inspections during 1997–1998 led to growing congressional calls for overthrowing Saddam Hussein, despite the perceived weaknesses of the Iraqi exiled opposition. A clear indication of congressional support for a more active US overthrow effort was encapsulated in a bill introduced in 1998—the Iraq Liberation Act (ILA) and signed into law on October 31, 1998.[5] The ILA gave the President authority to provide up to $97 million in defense articles to opposition organizations to be designated by the

Administration. The Act's passage was widely interpreted as an expression of congressional support for the concept of promoting an insurgency by using US air-power to expand opposition-controlled territory. This idea was advocated by Chalabi and some US experts. President Clinton signed the legislation despite reported widespread doubts within the Clinton Administration about the chances of success in promoting an opposition insurgency. In mid-November 1998, President Clinton publicly articulated that regime change was a component of US policy toward Iraq.

The signing of the ILA and the declaration of the overthrow policy came at the height of the one-year series of crises over UN weapons inspections in Iraq, in which inspections were repeatedly halted and restarted after mediation by the United Nations, Russia and others. On December 15, 1998, UN inspectors were withdrawn for the final time and a three-day US and British bombing campaign against suspected Iraqi WMD facilities followed—Operation Desert Fox, December 16–19, 1998.

The First ILA Designations

Further steps to promote regime change followed Operation Desert Fox. On February 5, 1999, after consultations with Congress, the President stated that the following organizations would be eligible to receive US military assistance under the Iraq Liberation Act: the INC, the INA, SCIRI, the KDP, the PUK, the Islamic Movement of Iraqi Kurdistan (IMIK), and the Movement for Constitutional Monarchy (MCM, see below). However, because of its possible role in contributing to the formation of Ansar al-Islam, the IMIK did not receive US support after 2001, although it was not formally taken off the ILA eligibility list.

[85]

Monarchists: Sharif Ali

The MCM, which was an original designee of eligibility to receive assistance under the ILA, is not likely to be a major factor is post-Saddam Iraq. It is led by Sharif Ali bin Al-Hussein, a relative of the Hashemite monarchs (he is a cousin of King Faysal II, the last Iraqi monarch) that ruled Iraq from the end of World War I until 1958. Sharif Ali, who is about 47 and was a banker in London, claims to be the leading heir to the former Hashemite monarchy, although there are other claimants, mostly based in Jordan. The MCM was considered a small movement that could not contribute much to the pre-war overthrow effort, although it was part of the INC and the United States had contact with it. In the post-war period, Sharif Ali returned to Iraq on June 10, 2003, to a small but apparently enthusiastic welcome. He did not participate in the major party grouping that negotiated with the US-led occupation authority on the formation of the Governing Council, and neither Sharif Ali nor any of his followers was appointed to the Governing Council.

Continued Doubts about the Capabilities of the Anti-Saddam Groups

In May 1999, in concert with an INC visit to Washington, the Clinton Administration announced it would provide $5 million worth of training and "non-lethal" defense equipment to the opposition, in accordance with the ILA. However, the Clinton Administration asserted that the opposition was not sufficiently organized to merit US provision of lethal military equipment or combat training. This restriction reflected divisions within and outside the Clinton Administration over the effectiveness and viability of the opposition and over the potential for the United States to become militarily embroiled in civil conflict in Iraq.

During 1999–2000, US efforts to rebuild and fund the anti-Saddam groups did not end the debate within the Clinton Administration over the regime change component of Iraq policy. Several members of Congress, from both political parties, expressed disappointment with the Clinton Administration's decision not to give the opposition lethal military aid or combat training. The Clinton Administration maintained that the Iraqi opposition would not succeed unless backed by direct US military involvement, and that direct US military action was risky and not justified by the degree of threat posed by Iraq. Others suggested the Clinton Administration should focus instead on rebuilding containment of Iraq by threatening force if Iraq refused to permit re-entry into Iraq of the UN weapons inspectors who had left Iraq in December 1998.

Bush Administration Policy

Bush Administration policy toward Iraq changed after the September 11, 2001 terrorist attacks, even though no evidence linking Iraq to those attacks came to light. The shift toward a more assertive policy first became clear in President Bush's State of the Union message on January 29, 2002, when he characterized Iraq as part of an "axis of evil," along with Iran and North Korea.

Pre-September 11 Policy

Throughout most of its first year, the Bush Administration continued the basic elements of Clinton Administration policy on Iraq. With no immediate consensus within the new Administration on how forcefully to proceed with an overthrow strategy, Secretary of State Powell focused on strengthening containment of Iraq, which the Bush Administration said had eroded substantially in the year prior to its taking office. Secretary Powell focused on obtaining UN approval of a so-called "smart sanctions" plan—a modification of the UN sanctions regime to ensure that no weapons-related technology reached Iraq.

Even though several senior officials had been strong advocates of a regime change policy, many of the questions about the wisdom and difficulty of that strategy that had faced previous administrations were debated early in the Bush Administration.[6] Aside from restating the US policy of regime change, the Bush Administration did little to promote that outcome throughout most of its first year. Like its predecessor, the Bush Administration initially declined to provide the opposition with lethal aid, combat training or a commitment of US military help.

Post-September 11: Moving to Change the Regime

Bush Administration policy toward Iraq became notably more assertive after the September 11, 2001 attacks, stressing regime change far more than containment. Almost immediately after the US-led war on the Taliban and al Qaeda in Afghanistan began in early October 2001, speculation began building that the Administration might try to change Iraq's regime through direct use of military force as part of a "phase two" of the war on terrorism. Some US officials reportedly believed that the United States needed to respond to the September 11 attacks by ending any or all regimes that support terrorist groups, including Iraq. Another view is that some of President Bush's advisers who had pushed for ousting Saddam at the end of the first Gulf War saw the September 11 attacks as an opportunity to implement their long held vision.

In his January 29, 2002 State of the Union message, President Bush named Iraq as part of the "axis of evil," along with North Korea and Iran. Vice President Cheney visited the Middle East in

March 2002 reportedly to consult regional countries about the possibility of confronting Iraq militarily, although the countries visited reportedly urged greater US attention to the Arab–Israeli dispute and opposed confrontation with Iraq.

The two primary themes in the Bush Administration's public case for confronting Iraq were, first, its refusal to verifiably end its WMD programs, and second, its ties to terrorist groups, to which Iraq might transfer WMD for the purpose of conducting a catastrophic attack on the United States. US officials said the September 11, 2001 attacks demonstrated that the United States could not wait for threats to gather before acting, but must instead act preemptively or preventively. The Administration added that regime change would have the further benefit of liberating the Iraqi people and promoting stability in the Middle East, possibly facilitating a resolution to the Arab–Israeli dispute.

Broadening the Internal Opposition to Saddam

As it began in mid-2002 to prepare for possible military action against Iraq, the Bush Administration tried to broaden and deepen its ties to Iraqi opposition groups and build up their capabilities. In early August 2002, the State and Defense Departments jointly invited the six major opposition groups with which the United States had worked since the end of the 1991 Gulf War – the INC, the INA, the KDP, the PUK, SCIRI, and the MCM – to Washington for meetings with senior officials, including a video link to Vice President Cheney. The meetings were held to show unity within the opposition and among different agencies of the US government, which reportedly tended to favor different opposition groups.

In addition, the Administration expanded its ties to Shiite Islamist groups and to groups composed of ex-military and security officers, as well as to some ethnic-based groups. The groups and individuals with which the Bush Administration had increasing contact during this period (mid-late 2002) include the following:

- Iraqi National Movement – formed in 2001 as an offshoot of the INC. Its leaders include ex-senior military officer Hassan Al-Naqib, who was part of an early leadership body of the INC.

- Iraqi National Front – another grouping of ex-military officers, founded in March 2000 by Tawfiq Al-Yasseri, a Shiite Muslim ex-military officer who participated in the post-1991 Gulf War anti-Saddam uprisings.

- Iraqi Free Officers and Civilians Movement – established in 1996 by ex-military officer Najib Salhi. Salhi, who defected in 1995, had served in the Republican Guard.

- Higher Council for National Salvation – based in Denmark, it was established in August 2002, headed by Wafiq Al-Samarra'i, a former head of Iraqi military intelligence. Former Chief-of-Staff of Iraq's military (1980–1991) Nizar Al-Khazraji, who was based in Denmark since fleeing Iraq in 1996, may also be a member.

- Iraqi Turkomen Front – a small, ethnic Turkomen-based grouping, generally considered aligned with Turkish policy on Iraq. Turkomens number about 350,000 and live mainly in northern Iraq.

- The Islamic Accord of Iraq – based in Damascus, this is another Shiite Islamic Party, but it is considered substantially less pro-Iranian than SCIRI or the Da'wa Party. It is headed by Jamil Wakil, a follower of Ayatollah Shirazi, an Iranian cleric who was the spiritual leader of a group called the Islamic Front for the Liberation of Bahrain (IFLB, see above). The IFLB allegedly attempted to overthrow Bahrain's regime in the early 1980s.

- The Assyrian Democratic Movement (ADM) – an ethnic-based movement headed by Secretary-General Yonadam Yousif Kanna. Iraq's Assyrian community is based primarily in northern Iraq. There is a strong diaspora presence in the United States as well. Kanna is now on the Governing Council.

The Bush Administration applauded efforts during 2002 by the ex-military-led groups to coordinate with each other, with the INC and other groups. One such meeting, in July 2002 in London and jointly run with the INC, attracted over 70 ex-military-officers. However, since the regime vacated Baghdad on April 9, 2003, virtually none of the ex-military-led groups listed above has openly sought a major role in post-Saddam Iraq.

Pre-War Planning by the United States and Anti-Saddam Groups

As the prospects for military action against Iraq grew, the opposition began planning its role in the war and the post-war period. During December 14–17, 2002, with US officials attending, the major Iraqi opposition groups held a conference in London and discussed whether the opposition should declare a provisional government. The Administration opposed that step on the grounds that doing so would give the impression that outside powers were determining Iraq's political structure and would be weighted toward exile groups. The meeting ended with agreement to form a 65-member "follow-up committee," which some criticized as weighted heavily toward Shiite Islamist groups such as SCIRI. The opposition met again during February 24–27, 2003, in northern Iraq, and formed, against the urging of US representatives at the meeting, a six seat "leadership committee" to prepare for a transition regime.

[91]

Again, due to Bush Administration opposition, the assembled groups did not declare a provisional government. The six-person leadership committee included PUK leader Jalal Talabani, KDP leader Masud Barzani, SCIRI leader Mohammed Baqr Al-Hakim, Ahmad Chalabi, INA leader Iyad Al-Alawi, and a former Iraqi foreign minister Adnan Pachachi. Today, all six groups of these personalities, or their designated representatives, are part of the rotating presidency of the Governing Council.

Decision to Take Military Action

As UN weapons inspectors (UN Monitoring, Verification, and Inspection Commission, UNMOVIC) led by Hans Blix, worked in Iraq under the new mandates provided in Resolution 1441, the Administration demanded complete disarmament and full cooperation if Iraq wanted to avert military action. The possibility of war became clearer following the mid-March 2003 breakdown of UN diplomacy over whether the UN Security Council should authorize war. The breakdown followed several briefings for the UN Security Council by Blix and the Director of the International Atomic Energy Agency (IAEA), Mohamed ElBaradei, the latest of which was on March 7, 2003. The Blix/ElBaradei briefings said Iraq had not accounted for its past WMD, but the two did not state that they were certain that Iraq had retained WMD, or that they had uncovered any banned WMD.

Security Council opponents of war, including France, Russia, China and Germany, said the briefings indicated that inspections should be given more time, and they argued that Iraq was well contained by sanctions and the US/British-enforced no-fly zones. They also maintained that, as long as Iraq allowed access to UN weapons inspections under Resolution 1441, Iraq could not pose an immediate threat to US national security. Other experts believed that, even if Iraq were to acquire major new WMD capabilities, Iraq could be deterred by US overall strategic superiority, presumably including the US nuclear arsenal.

The Administration asserted on March 17, 2003, that diplomatic options to disarm Iraq peacefully had failed and turned its full attention to military action. That evening, President Bush gave Saddam Hussein and his sons, Uday and Qusay, an ultimatum to leave Iraq within 48 hours to avoid war. They refused the ultimatum, and Operation Iraqi Freedom was launched on March 19, 2003.

In the war, Iraq's conventional military forces were overwhelmed by US and British forces in Operation Iraqi Freedom, although the Iraqi military, at times, put up stiff resistance using unconventional tactics. No major Iraqi military commanders or Baathist political figures came forward to try to establish a post-Saddam government, and senior regime leaders fled Baghdad. Much of the top leadership has since been captured, including Saddam Hussein, who was captured on December 13, 2003.

Post-War Political Scenarios

The outcome of a post-war debate on the results of the war might depend on such factors as the pace of reconstruction; the degree of resistance to the US-led occupation; the amount of WMD ultimately found, if any; and whether a new government is stable and democratic. These questions have now become part of the debate among Democratic candidates seeking to run against President Bush in the November 2004 US presidential elections.

Since Saddam Hussein's regime vacated Baghdad on April 9, 2003, the same US concerns about fragmentation of and instability in Iraq that existed since early 1991 have resurfaced. Although some Iraqi civilians have welcomed US and British troops in areas captured, many Iraqis now want US and British forces to leave Iraq. At the same time, it is likely that post-war Iraq will inevitably fall under the control of pro-Iranian Shiite Islamist forces who are asserting growing control over areas inhabited by Iraq's Shiites. This is an outcome which the Bush Administration is trying to prevent, for fear of strengthening Tehran and of creating a public impression that the war resulted in the establishment of a government similar to that of Iran. Shiites constitute about 60% of Iraq's population but have been under-represented in every Iraqi government since modern Iraq's formation in 1920, and even before that during Ottoman rule.

Establishing Iraqi Self-Rule

The Administration says that US forces will stay in Iraq until there is a stable, democratic successor regime. However, there has been some debate between US authorities, key anti-Saddam groups and US allies over the pace at which to move Iraq to self-government. Senior US officials, including Deputy Defense Secretary Paul Wolfowitz, said in early April 2003 that they hoped to have a successor regime in place within six months of the fall of the regime. However, in mid-May 2003, US officials, apparently fearing that existing major groups could not form a stable regime, or that Shiite Islamists would dominate, backed away from any deadlines for establishing an Iraqi self-rule authority.

Shortly after the war, the United States began a process of establishing a successor regime. The Administration organized an April 15 meeting, in Nasiriyah, of about 100 Iraqis of varying ideologies. However, SCIRI, along with several Shiite clerics that have appropriated authority throughout much of southern Iraq since the fall of the regime, boycotted the meeting and called for an

Islamic state and the withdrawal of US forces. Another meeting of about 250 delegates was held in Baghdad on April 26, ending in agreement to hold a broader meeting, within a month, to name an interim Iraqi Administration. That meeting was never held, as the process begun at the Nasiriyah meeting was cut short in May 2003 by a US decision to delay self-rule.

In parallel with the April 26 meeting, the five most prominent exiled opposition groups met, with US envoys present: SCIRI, the INC, the INA, the PUK and the KDP. On May 9, 2003, the five major parties agreed to expand their grouping to seven, adding to their ranks the little known Nasir Al-Chadirchy, head of a party called the National Democratic Party of Iraq, as well as the Shiite Islamist Da'wa Party. When the US decided in mid-May 2003 to delay self-rule, it was the seven member "major party grouping" that strongly criticized the US decision. The major party grouping subsequently began meeting with US occupation authorities to try to reverse that decision.

With US casualties in Iraq mounting and a growing sense of resentment among the Iraqi population, the US-led occupation authority (Coalition Provisional Authority, CPA) incorporated the views of the major party grouping. In late June, US administrator for Iraq Paul Bremer appeared to again shift US policy by saying that a planned advisory body of 25 to 30 Iraqi members would have "real authority" from its first days, including powers to nominate ministry heads, recommend policies and oversee a process for drafting a new constitution.[7]

The Governing Council

On July 13, 2003, the Governing Council was unveiled to the Iraqi public, appointed by the CPA but reflecting the influence of the seven-party grouping, as well as prominent Iraqis who were never in exile and were not affiliated with the exiled opposition. The Council has 25 members, of which 3 are women and 13 are Shiite Muslims.

Of the 13 Shiite Muslims on the Council, one seat is held by SCIRI directly (Abdul Aziz Al-Hakim, younger brother of Mohammed Baqr), one is held by a guerrilla affiliated with SCIRI (Abdul Karim Mohammedawi), two are Da'wa Party leaders (Ibrahim Al-Jafari and Abdul Zahra Othman) and considered allies of SCIRI, and one is a former Da'wa activist (Muwaffaq Al-Ruba'i). Also on the Council is a moderate Shiite cleric, Mohammed Bahr Al-Ulum, considered pro-US and not affiliated with SCIRI or the Da'wa. He headed the Ahl al-Bayt charity center in London from the 1980s. The remaining Shiite Muslims, such as Chalabi and Iyad Al-Alawi, are secular. Appointed to the Council was one Sunni Muslim Islamist, Muhsin Abdul Hamid, who heads the Iraqi Islamic Party (IIP). The Council includes five Kurds, including the two main Kurdish leaders Jalal Talabani and Masud Barzani. The Kurds are generally considered pro-US and might be expected to vote the way the US-led coalition wants.

Although not a cohesive bloc, the Council includes exiles and non-exiles who generally want a liberal democracy and would be considered pro-US. Most prominent among them is Chalabi, but this grouping includes National Democratic Party leader Nasir Al-Chadirchy and former foreign minister Adnan Pachachi, both of whom are Sunni Muslims, as well as former foreign ministry official Akila Al-Hashimi, a secular Shiite woman. Others most likely to affiliate with this bloc include Sunni businessman Samir Shakir Al-Sumaidy; Sunni civil engineer Ghazi Al-Yawar, who is president of Saudi-based Hicap Technology; the Shiite coordinator for the Human Rights Association of Babel, Ahmad Al-Barak; and the two other women Council members—Songul Chapouk, a Turkomen who heads the Iraqi Women's Association, and Raja Al-Khuza'i, a Shiite who heads the maternity hospital in Diwaniyah.

Yonadam Kanna, a member of the Assyrian Christian community is on the Council. He is the Secretary General of the Assyrian Democratic Movement (ADM). It is reasonable to believe that he has an affinity for fellow residents of northern Iraq, the Kurds. It is not yet clear whether or not Hamid Al-Musa, the Shiite head of the Iraqi Communist Party, is allied with anyone else on the Council.

In late July 2003, the Council decided that nine Council members will rotate as chairpersons, each for one month. Ibrahim Al-Jafari of the Da'wa Party was the first chairman, followed by Chalabi as chairman for the month of September. The other seven rotating chairpersons are Al-Alawi of the INA, Al-Hakim of SCIRI, Pachachi, Barzani of the KDP, Talabani of the PUK, Bahr Al-Ulum, and Abdul Hamid, the Sunni Islamist figure.

Among its first actions, the Council authorized the establishment of an Iraqi war crimes tribunal for Saddam and associates accused of major human rights abuses. It empowered a three-member delegation to seek formal UN recognition; Chalabi, Pachachi and Akila Al-Hashimi traveled to the United Nations in July 2003 and received a supportive statement from Secretary General Kofi Annan. No decision on seating the Governing Council at the United Nations was announced. Some Council members visited the Gulf monarchy states in August 2003 to expand the Council's regional profile. In early August 2003, the Governing Council appointed INC activist Kanaan Makiya to head a 25-person committee that would determine the process for drafting the constitution. In early

September 2003, Bremer laid out a seven point plan for returning Iraq to self-rule, including the possibility of national elections within about one year (summer of 2004).

On September 3, 2003, the Council took a major step by naming a 25-member cabinet whose factions and ethnicities mirror those of the Council itself. Among prominent figures, KDP activist Hoshyar Zebari was named Foreign Minister. Bahr Al-Ulum's son was named Oil Minister.

Post-War US Operations and the Resistance

Experts note that projections about US operations in post-war Iraq, including the duration of the US military occupation and the numbers of occupation troops, are largely dependent on the amount of continuing Iraqi resistance, the number of US casualties taken, and the rate at which such US objectives as the establishment of a stable and democratic successor regime are accomplished. At present, about 150,000 US, British and other troops remain in Iraq; of those, about 130,000 are US personnel and 11,000 are British. There are another approximately 10,000 foreign forces, deploying in accordance with international commitments to post-war peacekeeping.

The Resistance

The resistance could become a major political player in post-war Iraq. With the defeat of Saddam Hussein's regime, Sunni Muslims are largely leaderless. To preserve their influence in a post-Saddam Iraq, Sunnis will likely look to the resistance for leadership or to Sunni Islamist clerics who might be sympathetic to al Qaeda, or still to foreign volunteers fighting the occupation. Other Sunnis might look to the US-led occupation to protect their interests in post-war Iraq.

There are indications that resistance to the US governance of Iraq is becoming more multi-dimensional, judging by the frequency and form of recent attacks. The new Central Command (Centcom) commander John Abizaid said on July 17, 2003, that the United States faces a "classic guerrilla war" led by "mid-level Baath Party activists organized regionally." An apparent terrorist component to the resistance emerged in August 2003, with car/truck bombings in Baghdad of the embassy of Jordan on August 7, UN headquarters at the Canal Hotel on August 19, and the mosque of Ali in Najaf on August 29. The UN bombing killed 23 persons including the UN representative in Iraq, Sergio Vieira de Mello, and prompted some drawdown in UN and non-governmental organization personnel in Iraq; the Najaf bombing killed about 100, including Ayatollah Mohammed Baqr Al-Hakim.

The Bush Administration says resistance comes not only from remnants of the Baath Party but also from Arab volunteers, possibly linked to or supportive of al Qaeda, who have come to Iraq from other countries. Attacks have been more frequent in the Sunni areas of central Iraq, where support for Saddam Hussein's regime was traditionally stronger than elsewhere, but there have been fatal attacks in the Shiite areas in and around Basra. Some elements of the resistance appear to want to restore the old regime, while others appear to be motivated by opposition to foreign rule or the goal of forming an Islamic state. Other resistance fighters appear to be motivated by the difficulty the US and British authorities have had in restoring civilian services.

US military officials put the resistance numbers at about 5,000, although they do not explain precisely how they arrive at that figure. The resistance appears to be operating in relatively small cells, some of which have broadcast photos of armed fighters. Resistance factions have begun identifying themselves as distinct groups, scribbling graffiti warnings and faxing statements to the Arab satellite television network Al Jazeera, to Al Arabiya TV based in the United Arab Emirates (UAE) and other outlets. Suggesting a mix of Baathist and Islamists, resistance groups are using such names as:

- Al Awda (the Return)

- the Snakes

- the Movement of the Victorious Sect

- Iraq's Revolutionaries – Al Anbar's Armed Brigades

- the Popular Resistance for the Liberation of Iraq

- the Salafist Jihad Group (Salafi is a Sunni extremist Islamic movement)

- Armed Islamic Movement for al Qaeda – Falluja Branch; actual linkages to al Qaeda, if any, are not known.

- Jaysh (Army) of Mohammed

- Black Banners Group

- Nasirite Organization

- Armed Vanguard of the Second Mohammed Army, which claimed responsibility for the UN headquarters bombing and threatened attacks on any Arab countries that participate in Iraq peacekeeping; the credibility of the claim is not known.

Some Shiite factions are becoming more active against the occupation. The Sadr faction has reportedly instigated riots and demonstrations that took place against US and British forces in

Baghdad and Basra in August 2003. One report says that Sunni Islamists, led by Sheikh Ahmad Qubaysi, who returned in April 2003 from exile in a neighboring country, is assisting the Sadr faction.[8] This represents the possible emergence of a Sunni-Shiite Islamist anti-occupation coalition.

The continuing resistance has complicated the US mission. In addition to targeting US forces, resistance fighters have assassinated Iraqis who are cooperating with the United States and attacked oil export pipelines and water and other infrastructure facilities. By attacking these targets, the resistance appears to be hoping to slow reconstruction and thereby turn the Iraqi populace against the occupation. On the other hand, the Administration maintains that reconstruction is proceeding apace and has logged a number of major accomplishments, as discussed in a White House fact sheet.[9]

Building Security Institutions

While attempting to restore security to Iraq, the CPA is beginning to build new Iraqi institutions that can help secure major facilities and leave the US forces available to combat the resistance. The United States is planning to train a 40,000 person Iraqi army, about 10% the size of the pre-war Iraqi force. About 12,000 are expected to be in the force by mid-2004.

The CPA is also trying to turn basic policing functions over to Iraqis. Overall, about 40,000 Iraqi policemen have returned to their jobs, more than half the total goal of 65,000 nationwide, expected to be reached some time in 2004. The CPA is also recruiting a 7,000 strong all-Iraqi civil defense force to guard installations such as oil pumping stations, electricity substations and like facilities.

[101]

Expanding the International Role in Peacekeeping and Governance

The relatively slow pace of establishing Iraqi security institutions, coupled with ongoing security difficulties and continued US casualties, has led to calls from members of Congress and others for the Administration to expand its efforts to enlist other countries to help with the stabilization of Iraq. The continuing inability of US forces to secure all of Iraq, coupled with the continued sabotage, has led to widespread assessments that the US occupation is in difficulty. As of late August, following the several car bombings noted above, negotiations have accelerated with other countries on a possible UN-authorized multinational peacekeeping force in Iraq. This has been accompanied by numerous press reports indicating that President Bush has given greater authority over post-war Iraq policy to Secretary of State Powell, and possibly curbed the influence of the Defense Department, which has thus far controlled post-war Iraq policy. Many Administration critics blame civilian leaders in the Defense Department for overly optimistic assumptions about post-war Iraq that have led to the current difficulties.

Supporters of the Administration say that the occupation is already multilateral. According to the Administration, more than 30 countries are already supplying forces for a multilateral stabilization force. The United Kingdom and Poland are leading multinational divisions in that mission in southern Iraq and central Iraq, respectively. However, the commitments of several large nations, including Germany, France, India and Turkey appear contingent on a new UN resolution formally authorizing a multilateral force and altering the international presence from a US-led occupation to an international stabilization operation, which would possibly include dismantling the Coalition Provisional Authority. These larger nations might be capable of supplying as many as 10,000 troops apiece, and their decision to participate in post-war peacekeeping could potentially enable the United States to bolster security in Iraq while drawing down its own forces substantially.

However, there have been numerous reports that the Administration does not want to agree to a UN resolution that dilutes its prerogatives in Iraq, particularly its authority in determining a new political structure. Opponents of ceding authority maintain that UN control could facilitate the rise to power in Iraq of a government that is not to US liking. Others believe that the United States must share authority with the United Nations, if the United States is to be able to wind down the occupation of Iraq. It is likely that, to head off continued casualties that appear to be reducing US public support for the US effort in Iraq, the Bush Administration will agree to a compromise that cedes substantial authority to the United Nations and the international community.

Conclusion

The Bush Administration has been hesitant to cede authority over post-Saddam Iraq to the United Nations or those Iraqis whom it has backed against Saddam since the first Gulf War. However, continued instability in Iraq, a growing resistance and escalating occupation costs appear to be compelling the Administration to give up some of its control in exchange for spreading the burden of peacekeeping. It is hoped that turning over greater responsibility to Iraqi groups and the international community could allow the United States to draw down substantial numbers of its forces still in Iraq.

One major consideration the Administration has in calibrating the scope of its authority is its goal of preventing the formation of a

Shiite Islamist-led state in post-war Iraq. The Administration apparently fears that ceding responsibility could bring about that result. However, it is almost inevitable that Shiite Islamist parties will achieve political dominance in post-war Iraq, particularly Arab Iraq, if not in the Kurdish controlled north. The Shiite Islamists have a well developed leadership structure capable of imposing a measure of discipline on the numerically dominant Shiite Muslim community of Iraq, and the ability to mobilize overwhelmingly large numbers of Iraqis in political shows of strength.

The dominance of Iraq by Shiite Islamist groups will no doubt strengthen the hand of Tehran in Iraq and in the region. Tehran has long nurtured and supported Iraqi Shiite Islamist groups, and has extensive ties to and influence over them. However, the Shiite Islamist groups are conscious of Iraqi nationalism, and are unlikely to follow Tehran's dictates blindly. Iraqi Shiite Islamists are unlikely to try to form an exclusively Shiite state modeled on Iran's Islamic republic; the Iraqi Shiite Islamist parties have cultivated extensive ties to Iraq's Sunni Arab and Kurdish communities and are unlikely to seek to rule these communities through suppression. The emerging strength of Iraqi Shiites is also likely to embolden Shiite movements throughout the region, including in the Gulf and in Lebanon.

Islamist Politics in Iraq after the Fall of Saddam

Graham Fuller

O vert Islamist politics played almost no role in Iraq during the era of Baath Party rule. The rule of Saddam did not permit opposition movements of any kind to exist in the county and he dealt ruthlessly with any potential challenge, including from Islamists.

This reality is striking because the absence of Islamist politics in Iraq has constituted an extraordinary exception to the pattern we witness in most other Muslim countries where Islamists dominate the political opposition. This paper will briefly:

- look at the reasons for the prominence of Islamist movements in the Muslim world;

- examine the ways in which Islamist movements may now play a role in the new post-Saddam Iraq; and

- speculate on the implications of Islamist politics in Iraq for Iraq's future relations in the region.

Islamism in the Muslim World

It is useful to review the role of Islamist parties in the Muslim world more broadly in order to discern what patterns might apply to the future of Iraqi politics as well.

What is an Islamist?

First of all, a definition of Islamism, or political Islam is required. Islam is of course a religion. However, political Islam represents the attempt to apply the principles and teachings of Islam to political and social organization within Muslim societies and states. An Islamist is anyone who works to implement these beliefs in the political sphere through political or social organization.

Is Osama bin Laden an Islamist? Indeed he is, for he attempts to change the world according to his understanding of Islam. Nevertheless, this does not at all mean that all Islamists are terrorists or necessarily violent. Examples of other Islamists are those who run the current regime in Sudan, and in Iran, both quite different from each other. The same name can be ascribed to the Muslim Brotherhood (al-Ikhwan al-Muslimin), a huge and now non-violent movement in Egypt, as well as the 30 million strong organizations of the Nahdatul Islam and Muhammadiyah movements in Indonesia. A further example is the ruling party in Turkey (2003–2004), the Justice and Development Party, which is a highly moderate party with Islamist roots that seeks entry into the European Union and cooperates well with the United States. The Tablighi Jamaat in Pakistan is also an Islamist grouping, which seeks to change the world through mass organization but without direct political action.

In other words, what we are talking about is a broad and expanding spectrum of groups, movements and parties across the

[106]

Muslim world. Although this spectrum includes violent, radical, traditional and anti-democratic elements, it weighs more heavily on the side of non-violent, moderate, modernist and pro-democratic individuals and groups. Thus, Islamist groupings are neither unified nor monolithic. Indeed, they do not even agree on goals or methods. There are broad differences among them, and some are hostile to each other. This is not surprising because the Koran and the Hadith (the sayings and actions of the Prophet) offer no clear political blueprint for any kind of political organization. They offer only a few broad principles and values of politics and society, which human beings must then interpret for themselves and implement according to their understanding in each age and according to the conditions they live in.

The Success of Political Islam

Political Islam today, in all its various movements, represents the largest and most important opposition force across the Muslim world. Although varying from country to country, generally, political Islam has few serious rivals—be it from nationalists, leftists or liberals. Political Islam owes part of its success to the fact that in the majority of Muslim countries the regimes in power have banned *all* political parties. Since the Islamists operate from the mosque and the neighborhood, and have deep grass roots, they are able to organize politically in ways that most other parties cannot. To the extent that any political currents of opposition existed within Saddam's Iraq, these were mostly underground movements formed by some Islamists.

After Saddam's disastrous setback in the 1991 Gulf War over Kuwait, he began to encourage a more pious and Islamic image in order to gain greater support from the people. Even before 1991, he had opened hundreds of new mosques in the country and established a major new theological school called Saddam University that taught only the Sunni version of Islamic theology which included many of the writings of classic Islamists, enabling its graduates to gain some understanding of contemporary Islamist thinking. Saddam himself sought to exhibit personal piety at public prayer, and even emblazoned the Islamic invocation "there is no god but God" onto the Iraqi national flag. In his new emphasis on public observation of Islam, he also closed down dancing clubs, casinos and bars. Twelve tame Islamic scholars were appointed into the Iraqi rubber-stamp parliament. Public observation of Islam, however, rigorously excluded any hint of political activity or of Islamist activity.[1]

In the six month run-up to the US attack on Iraq in 2003, Saddam began to ease off on persecution of known members of the Brotherhood, ostensibly out of fear that the movement had deep roots in Iraqi society and should not be gratuitously alienated at a time of regime crisis, particularly among his core source of support, the Sunni Arabs.[2]

It is of course, notoriously difficult to judge the level and depth of Brotherhood supporters within Iraq during this period of harsh regime crackdown on all political opposition. Any such activity was underground and known best only to the security organs of the regime itself. Nonetheless, given the strength of the Brotherhood in other Arab states – neighboring Syria, Jordan, in Egypt and in the Gulf – it is highly likely that the nucleus of an underground Brotherhood remained in place, now free to emerge. The Muslim Brotherhood in exile also claimed that it smuggled political and religious materials into the country during this period.

Many of the movements of political Islam also have international ties, which help them to organize and develop programs and strengthen their position. The Muslim Brotherhood is the largest such organization, with links across most of the Muslim world, even though the conditions and leaderships differ considerably from place to place.

Islamist parties and movements also attempt to speak with a voice of cultural authenticity. Their programs are not direct reflections of foreign – especially Western – ideologies and structures, but seek to derive their values and principles out of Islam. When Muslim societies feel oppressed by Western power and intervention, they naturally often look to their own roots of Islam as an alternative. Since the terrorist events of September 11, 2001 in the United States and the subsequent global war against terrorism, the Muslim world has indeed felt under siege, which has strengthened the forces of opposition to Western intrusion, particularly among Islamists. When faced with foreign non-Muslim threats, Islamists tend to act much as do nationalists—focusing on defense of the homeland in the name of Muslim culture. Under these conditions, they also cooperate with nationalists, as we can see today in Iraq.

Islamists also provide a serious critique of existing regimes in the Muslim world, focusing on the fact that most are illegitimate – that is, not elected by the people – are often incompetent, corrupt and weak in defending the interests of their own countries in the face of Western power. In this context, it is notable that the legitimately elected Islamist government in Turkey in 2003 felt able to successfully deny the US the right to use Turkey as a military base for the war against Saddam. The US was compelled to accept this reality because it reflected public opinion in Turkey. At the same time most Arab rulers felt so insecure as to be unable or unwilling to say no the US. Islamists have always had strong criticisms of the nature of the Saddam regime—its illegitimacy, its brutality and corruption, even if it did stand up to the West.

Islamism and the Fall of Saddam

The totalitarian nature of the Baath party in Iraq did not permit any significant presence or activity by Islamist movements inside Iraq. However, with the fall of the Baath regime and the return to a more open form of government and society – even under American occupation – why should Iraq remain an exception to the general phenomenon of a major role for Islamist movements inside Arab and Muslim states? It did not require much imagination to assume that Islamist politics would rapidly appear in the new Iraq.

Indeed, there are some important additional reasons why Islamist movements would become important inside Iraq after the political scene opened up in the post-Saddam era. One is the particularly sectarian (ta'ifi) nature of Iraq society, with its divisions into Shiite and Sunni communities, in which approximately 60 percent of the country are Shia. Because of these religious divisions the sectarian community, either Shia or Sunni, often forms the basis for some political activity.

Sectarianism in Iraq

It is important to recognize here that sectarianism is not the sole basis of Iraqi political and social organization and orientation. During most periods in Iraqi history, particularly after the establishment of a new independent Iraqi state, Shiites and Sunnis cooperated within the social system and sectarian differences were minimized. Social interaction between Shia and Sunnis was broad and included frequent marriages across sectarian lines. This was especially true in the sophisticated city of Baghdad where Shias and

Sunnis are more or less equally represented. Thus, there is no inherent hostility between the two groups at the social level.

Nonetheless, for most of Iraqi history, including under the Ottomans and later the Baath party, political power has remained primarily within the hands of the Sunni Arab minority, some 20 percent of the population. The Shia largely focused on commerce and agriculture.

Baath rule, particularly under Saddam's tactics of divide and rule, created far greater divisiveness within Iraqi society, and each community tended to turn in upon itself for solidarity and protection. It was the Shia, in particular, who rose up against Saddam's rule after the end of the Gulf War in 1991, at the urging of George Bush senior, and who were then slaughtered when they were offered no protection by American forces. Saddam viewed the Shia – as well as the Kurds – as inherently disloyal and untrustworthy, leading further to their isolation.

Thus, while sectarian divisions and rivalries need not be the dominant force within Iraqi society and politics, at present they are strong forces due to the Baathi legacy. Regrettably sectarian politics within Iraq today are probably stronger than ever and represent – along with Kurdish ethnicity – the key vehicle for political rivalry. This trend is likely to increase for a certain period into the future as the Shia move more aggressively into the political arena for the first time in centuries, apart from an abortive effort to achieve major voice at the time of resistance to the British protectorate. Sectarian (Sunni–Shiite) and ethnic (Arab–Kurd) politics need not represent the permanent future of Iraqi politics.

Nevertheless, today each of these three major elements within the country is fighting to establish a clear position for itself within the newly emerging system and will seek to enshrine its political aspirations and key demands within a new constitution and in the new institutions of government. Perhaps after the formation of a new Iraqi political order, politics will gradually become more "normal" and will demonstrate other social patterns of organization – ideological, regional, professional or class – more typical of other states.

Islamism among the Shia

The existence of the Shiite community goes back as far as the death of the Prophet Mohammed when dispute broke out over whether his successor should be hereditary, as the Shia called for, or selected from among pious and virtuous followers, which was the Sunni desire. Since that time, a whole separate body of lore, history, literature, culture, traditions, philosophy and jurisprudence has developed over centuries within the Shiite community, even though basic Islamic theology differs very little between the two sects. However, the Shiite community, by definition, is defined by religion – and now by history and identity – but not by ethnicity. Religion constitutes its very raison d'être.

In this sense, it is difficult to be a "secular Shia." Of course any individual Shiite may not be religious, but that person is still born as a member of a religious community in terms of family and social ties and is generally viewed by non-Shia in religious terms as "Shia." Many Shia who seek to be modern and "Iraqi first" in their identity can still be frustrated when others continue to see them as Shiite, and perhaps even to make political and social calculations towards them on that basis. In other words, it is difficult to abandon the community connection, even if one seeks to do so. It's interesting to note in this context that many Shia joined the Iraqi Communist Party over the past five decades in Iraq, primarily because it was the one political party that had absolutely no interest in the ethnic or religious origin of its members. Arab nationalist parties or the Baath were strongly Sunni in flavor and hence presented a less sympathetic environment for Shiites.

Finally, the power of the clergy within the Shiite community is a major factor in Shiite politics. Senior clerics – ayatollahs and other *maraji' al-taqlid* (literally "sources of emulation") – have always played the dominant leadership roles for the community. This does not mean that the Shia wish to have an Islamic state in which clerics rule (*wilayat al-Faqih*) as in Iran. In fact, the Iranian system as first established by Khomeini was a considerable innovation in Shiite history, not accepted by all Shiite clerics by any means. The role of the clerics traditionally had been to stand outside the political order and to serve as moral guides and commentators, passing judgments on the Islamic correctness of certain laws or behaviors. They often were the key spokesmen for the community and its welfare, but rarely were they the actual administrators and rulers themselves. All along, they sought to preserve their moral purity by remaining outside the potentially corrupting nature of any political order of power.

It is important to remember here that, in general, ayatollahs are not appointed through some political process. They owe their leadership position within the community to the prestige gained among the community through their actions and the number of their followers. An ayatollah gains his position slowly over the years as individuals choose that cleric over another to be their *marja al-taqlid*, or source of emulation, the cleric whom they trust and wish to follow in his rulings on spiritual and even broad community issues. One may come from a line of distinguished ayatollahs, but each new aspirant must build his own following to attain real leadership—it does not come automatically. Thus, the legitimacy of most ayatollahs is powerful since it must be earned.

Today, there are several key clerical figures in the Iraqi Shiite community who represent the dominant voices in Shiite politics. The most important is Grand Ayatollah Ali Al-Sistani who belongs to the "quietist" tradition of Shiite politics, that is, minimal daily involvement in the give-and-take of politics but who does offer periodic opinions on key issues of the day. He is cautious and conservative rather than radical in approaching political issues. He cautioned his followers against acts of violence against the American occupation from the outset, even while making it clear that the Americans can have no role in determining the nature of the future constitution and government of Iraq. If defied on this important principle, it is quite conceivable that Al-Sistani could call upon his followers to resist the occupation authorities.

A second key ayatollah was Baqr Al-Hakim who was murdered towards the end of 2003 by a car bomb by unknown assailants. He came from a prominent family of ayatollahs who enjoy great respect among the Shia. Al-Hakim had close ties to Iran, where he had taken refuge from Saddam for many years, and was the founder of the Supreme Council for the Islamic Revolution in Iraq (SCIRI). This organization was based for a long period in Iran but through Baqr Al-Hakim it had also dealt with Washington for many years as part of the Iraqi National Council (INC) that was planning for the future of a new Iraq after the fall of Saddam. Al-Hakim was much more politically oriented than Al-Sistani, but despite his close ties with Iran, he did not represent the Iranian school of clerical rule. SCIRI continues as a major actor on the Shiite scene in Iraq, largely pragmatic in orientation, but definitely more political than Al-

Sistani. Ayatollah Baqr Al-Hakim was replaced within SCIRI by his brother Abdul Aziz Al-Hakim.

A far more controversial figure is Muqtada Al-Sadr, the youthful son of Sayyid Mohammed Sadiq Al-Sadr who was assassinated by Saddam in 1999, and relative of the great Iraqi jurist Ayatollah Mohammed Baqr Al-Sadr, who was executed by Saddam in 1980. Muqtada formed the Jama'at al-Sadr al-Thani (The Association of the Second al-Sadr) as the key organization of the Sadrists. Muqtada is a shadowy figure, reported as headstrong, inexperienced and clearly lacking any clerical credentials except as inheritor of family name. Muqtada himself is quite radical and opportunist and has delivered many fiery speeches against the American presence, subsequently toned down when threatened with arrest. He has furthermore issued statements insisting on the validity of his father's political rulings which, according to mainstream (Usuli) Shiite theology, should have lost its legal force upon the death of the issuer. Muqtada Al-Sadr verbally attacked Al-Sistani in April 2003 and for a brief period issued threats that Al-Sistani as well as two other leading clerics – Baqr Al-Hakim and Muhammad Ishaq Al-Fayyad – should leave the country, a call denounced by other leading Shiite clerics. There were press reports that Muqtada might have been behind the murder of Abdul Majid Al-Khoei, another younger cleric from a highly distinguished clerical family who was moderate and a respected leader of the Shiite community in the UK, where he was resident for many years. Al-Khoei was stabbed to death during a mob confrontation in April 2003. There are also suspicions that Muqtada Al-Sadr or his followers may have been behind the assassination of Ayatollah Baqr Al-Hakim.

Meanwhile, the Sadrists maintain dominance among the large Shiite community in Baghdad's massive "Sadr City" (the former

"Saddam City.") Muqtada is largely ignored by the leading Shiite clerics in the country. Sadr's authority derives from the power of the family name and tradition, and from his influence within Sadr City, but his influence is almost exclusively political and not founded on any religious prestige. His following derives from his political positions and actions and not from religious legitimacy. Nonetheless, this kind of power cannot be discounted in its ability to roil the waters during a delicate period of transition.

Al-Sadr has raised the issue of "foreign origin" of several key Shiite clerics in Iraq, including Al-Sistani (Iranian origin), Muhammad Ishaq Al-Fayyad (Afghan) and Bashir Najafi (Pakistani). These charges are politically significant in that they represent a major effort to promote a "nativist" approach to Shiite politics in Iraq that casts doubts on the appropriateness of religious leaders not of Iraqi blood. In religious terms, this should not be an issue. Furthermore, given the cultural intermixing between Iran and Iraq over history, it is hard to find such a thing as a "pure Iraqi." Furthermore, there is no "ethnic tradition" within political Islam in general. Iraqi Shiite leaders will aspire for influence among all Shiites in the Muslim world and their specific ethnic origin should not be a significant factor. It remains to be seen how effectively Muqtada will be able to wield this issue as a way of diminishing the prestige of major ayatollahs; the chances are that it will not be of great significance unless tensions with Iran should rise.

An additional important Islamist force among the Iraqi Shia is the Da'wa (Call to Islam) Party, probably the oldest Shiite Islamist movement in Iraq, dating back to 1957 in Najaf, when it called for the establishment of an Islamic state. This radical political agenda of al-Da'wa represented a revolutionary turning point in the highly conservative environment in the Shiite holy city of Najaf at the time.

The Da'wa rapidly achieved prominence through its use of violence against the Saddam regime starting in the 1970s and was ruthlessly repressed. Its boldness in attacking the regime and the price it paid in blood for this resistance earned the Da'wa a great deal of respect and legitimacy among Iraqi Shia. In the 1980s, it was galvanized by the Iranian revolution and was linked with other al-Da'wa branches in the Gulf, some of which committed a number of terrorist acts against existing regimes. The Da'wa ultimately split between a more Iranian-oriented faction and a more independent London-based branch that is more "Iraqi" in character and that has become much more moderate.

Both branches of the party have remained pragmatic about dealing with the realities of US power for the moment, but that tolerance may be short-lived if Shiites come to view the US presence as the chief barrier to assumption of greater national power by the Shia. The future role of the Da'wa is still uncertain since its earlier popularity and legitimacy may have diminished with time and new circumstances. It could, however, bid to be the major contender for a "nativist" Iraqi Shiite movement and could, therefore, join forces with the Sadrists, especially given the role of the Al-Sadr family in the movement in the past. The inclusion of al-Da'wa in the Governing Council of Iraq under US occupation could lead it in more moderate directions, compared to the excluded al-Sadr movement, but al-Da'wa remains a key unknown force for the future.

The Shiite community as a whole has been far more moderate towards the US occupation than have been the Sunnis, for several reasons. First, the Shiite community received the brunt of hostility and suffering from Saddam's Baath Party rule, while the Arab Sunnis tended to be the greater beneficiaries—even while suffering from Saddam's brutality and despotism themselves. Thus, the Shia, along with the Kurds, were the chief beneficiaries of Saddam's overthrow and grateful to the US that brought it about. Second, the Shia pin their hopes for future power in Iraq on their demographic dominance that will prevail in a future democratic order in the country. The US is formally committed to democracy in Iraq and the Shia do not wish to disrupt this US plan. They have therefore been willing to be patient with the US occupation, even while wishing it to bring about the democratization of Iraq as quickly as possible.

If the US plans for departure from Iraq appear to leave an unresolved political situation in which full democracy has not been attained, the Shiites will see themselves as facing once again possible marginalization in the coming political order. Under such circumstances they will resist US plans strongly and will feel compelled to enter the arena of militia power to face an unknown future that may be determined by armed conflict. Thus, Shiite forbearance towards the US presence is based strictly on a calculation that for now that presence serves Shiite interests. The situation could rapidly change.

In summary, not only are nearly all the major leaders within the Shiite community religious figures, but there is also some rivalry among them as they command different followings within the community and possess differing views on some of the key political issues of the day that affect the Muslim community. In this sense, political Islam is an inherent element within the Shiite community, even without full consensus—as is also the case among Sunni Islamists.

The Sunni Islamists

It is harder to analyze the nature of Sunni Islamist power in Iraq since, unlike the Shia who were always lead by prominent ayatollahs, the Sunni Islamists were not only heavily suppressed but were politically overshadowed by the powerful Sunni-based ruling Baath party.

Furthermore, the Sunni community is less integrally linked to religion in the political sphere than are the Shia. This is partly because in most of the Arab and Muslim world the Sunnis represent the majority—although not in Iraq. The Sunni Arab community is less defined by its Sunni religious character than are Shia with their close linkage to Shiism as the key element of identity. Furthermore, historically there have been important alternative movements within the Sunni world that were not religious—especially the force of Arab nationalist parties, of which the Baath was one. While Arab nationalism has no specific ties to Islam, it is implicitly "Sunni" in its view of the nature of Arab and Islamic history. Shia have rarely felt comfortable within the framework of Arab nationalist parties even though, in principle, such parties are secular. In Iraqi history, the great 'Abbasid Caliphate was of course Sunni and there is a tradition of great Sunni victories over the Shia and against the Shia of Iran.

It is less easy to find evidence of Sunni Islamist activity in Iraq under Saddam when the movement was fully suppressed. Nonetheless, after the fall of the Baath regime one could assume with some assurance that Sunni Islamism would return in full force to Iraq, just as it functions prominently in most other Arab countries.

As in most of the rest of the Arab world, the Muslim Brotherhood is the single most powerful and important Islamist movement in

[119]

Iraq. The Brotherhood, as a movement that is widely represented across most of the Arab world, stems from the earliest tradition of modern Islamist politics that began in Egypt in the 1920s under Hasan Al-Banna and Sayyid Qutb, two seminal Egyptian thinkers on political Islam. The Brotherhood in Egypt, after practising political violence in its early decades, gave up political violence and became a mainstream Islamist movement, less literalist, more tolerant and less xenophobic than the Saudi-based Wahhabi tradition, which today is a rival to the Brotherhood. An exception is Hamas in Palestine—an armed wing of the Palestinian Brotherhood, which itself eschewed political violence until the 1980s and the beginning of the first *intifada* during which it felt it could not allow itself be eclipsed by secular Palestinian guerrilla organizations in the cause of national liberation.

The Brotherhood in Iraq was officially founded in 1951 and from the outset had close ties with the Palestinian and Egyptian branches of the movement. Indeed, the Iraqi Brotherhood, from its earliest days, was concerned with the question of Palestine as representative of a foreign takeover of Muslim lands—an issue that will not fade from the movement's attention even today. The Brotherhood adopted the name of The Islamist Party of Iraq, a name it still retains. It propagated a basic message that the fundamental ills of the Muslim society are due to deviation from the teachings of Islam and that Muslim society can only be cured by a return to those same principles. While Western colonialism and imperialism was always a key target of the Brotherhood, it was actually the Communist Party that constituted the main rival and threat to the Brotherhood in terms of both power and challenge to the communists' atheist ideology.

In an early manifesto in 1960, the Muslim Brotherhood proclaimed the following principles:

- Muslims and non-Muslims must enjoy the same "political, public and individual rights;"

- A democratic order is required in which non-Muslims have the right to elect their own representatives and to vote for a [Muslim] President;

- The legal system should be neither Islamic nor positivist, but society should be ruled according to Sharia law.

- State land should go to the peasants;

- Women have the right to work;

- Trade unions should be established;

- National resources belong to the people;

- National unity must be upheld on the basis of common citizenship;

- National unity is the nucleus of a higher stage of Arab unity that in turn is the nucleus of overall Muslim unity.

- In global terms "the people of all nations are seen as integral parts of a united whole – humanity – irrespective of ethnic origin or religion."[3]

The Brotherhood leadership called for joint Sunni/Shiite membership within the Iraqi Islamic Party, but Sayyid Muhsin Al-Hakim, the ranking Shia cleric at the time, declined and forbade cooperation of Shia with the Party. It will be interesting to see whether such a call today between the Brotherhood and the Iraqi Shiite leadership will fall on more fertile ground.

With the fall of Baath Party rule, a struggle for power in the new Iraq has broken out. That struggle began under the US occupation but will focus primarily on the game after the withdrawal of US power and the establishment of a new sovereign Iraqi authority.

Neighboring states in the region cannot remain uninterested in the direction of events in post-Saddam Iraq. Indeed, there were press accounts after the fall of Baghdad that leading Iraqi Sunni clerics in exile had returned to Iraq to examine the situation for the Sunni Islamists there. These accounts suggested that Muslim Brotherhood forces in the region, and perhaps some neighboring Sunni states, were concerned about the status of Sunni Islamism in the new Iraq. This confirms to the informed observer the early re-emergence of Brotherhood power in Iraq, possibly in the context of a rivalry with Shiite Islamist power.

Radical Sunni Islamist Elements

Information is very sketchy about the presence of more radical Sunni Islamist forces in Iraq after the fall of Saddam. US occupation forces and other anecdotal sources frequently claim that some elements of international jihadists are also present in Iraq, often linked, perhaps erroneously, with al Qaeda. There can be little doubt that, after the fall of the Baath regime and the presence of a large US occupational force in Iraq, the new situation has attracted international jihadi forces who seek an opportunity to confront the US on the ground. Indeed, the US forces present an unusually attractive target since they can be engaged in guerrilla warfare in an urban environment, a far more level playing field than existed during formal military combat when US forces operated from far afield and utilized high technology weapons. It is not yet clear whether these guerrilla forces are weakening or diminishing, after the capture of Saddam Hussein, but the general logic of guerrilla conflict suggests that the opposition may continue to grow, even if it is not directly supported by most of the population.

In addition, any analyst of the Iraq situation would certainly expect a growth in the presence of Wahhabi-oriented clerics, perhaps directly from Saudi Arabia. These Wahhabi forces need not be violent, but are designed to strengthen the Saudi message in the country and to combat Shiite power, a leading Wahhabi goal. Indeed, some leading Wahhabi clerics in Saudi Arabia have called for a struggle against American occupation forces in order to liberate Iraq. The Muslim Brotherhood in Iraq shares the same long term goal of departure of US occupation forces, but also sees Wahhabi forces as rivals. The Brotherhood's longer term interests clash sharply with those of the radical jihadis, in terms of ideology, program, means and goals. In the end the moderate Sunni Islamists like the Brotherhood may be the most effective force in combating the radicals.

The Implications of Iraqi Islamism for Iraqi Foreign Policy

This paper posits that eventually Iraq will see the establishment of some kind of democratic order in which the Shia will represent the dominant, but not exclusive, voice. A major new Shiite input into Iraqi foreign policy represents an unprecedented development in the history of Iraq at any time and will have significant implications for the country's foreign policy, depending on the nature of the Shiite policies and leadership. These developments will also impact upon the entire region.

We cannot of course guess what kind of foreign policy line the new Iraq will adopt, and much depends upon the nature of the

[123]

sectarian balance and leadership in the country. However, it is unlikely that even a government with strong Shiite representation will suddenly switch to being a "Shiite state" or start pursuing a "Shiite foreign policy" as Iran did in its early years after the revolution. There is little doubt that Iraq will pursue a pragmatic policy in the interests of the state at large, one that seeks to be non-sectarian in its outlook. It will almost surely not allow the sectarian makeup of other countries to affect its treatment of them. Nevertheless, the mere fact that Iraq will have powerful Shiite representation in a new government will have direct impact on other states. Even without any direct statement of interest in the Shia elsewhere in the world, the new Iraqi state could make its preferences and concerns felt in indirect ways. At the level of civil society, unquestionably ayatollahs and civil society groups will speak out on Shiite world issues even if the formal government of Iraq does not. A subtle shift of sectarian power in the region will be felt, even if it is moderate and pragmatic.

Shiite Iraq and Iran

Iran is of course today the preeminent Shiite state in the world, in terms of size and influence. However, even though Shia have never dominated Iraq politically in the past, its holy sites, especially the cities of Najaf and Karbala have been vastly more important in the whole Shiite world than Qom, the chief seat of clerical rule in Iran. The two Iraqi cities were the seat of major Shiite institutions and schools of theology for many centuries. Indeed, Iran's Qom only attained its real religious prominence with the Iranian revolution and the eclipse of Najaf and Karbala under Saddam's anti-Shiite policies. The new Islamic Republic of Iran quickly sought to establish itself as the leader of the Shiite world, from India to North Africa, and in the heyday of its revolutionary fervor it stirred up much radical action among the Gulf Shiites. However, with the emergence of Shiite power in the new post-Saddam Iraq, Najaf and Karbala have both begun a process of restoration of their previous prominence and theological authority.

While Iran is pleased to see the downfall of Saddam Hussein, the hated rival and instigator of the devastating Iran–Iraq war in 1979, the reemergence of Shiite power and leadership in Iraq is not necessarily all good news for Iran. In fact, rather than arguing that Iran and Iraq will now cooperate to strengthen the power of Shiism in the Muslim world, the converse may well be more likely—a sharp rivalry between Iran and Iraq will rapidly emerge as Najaf and Karbala regain their earlier prominence and vie for influence across the Shiite world.

The rivalry will probably be both in theology as well as in political power. Since the revolution, Iran has championed Khomeini's somewhat novel idea of rule by Shiite clerics, while most of the prominent Shiite clerics in Iraq, even those who have worked with Tehran in the past, are less inclined to accept the concept of clerical rule, both because of its problems, and because Shiite clerical rule in Iraq would pose major problems to the 40 percent of the population that is not Shia. If leading Iraqi Shiite theologians reject Iran's principle of clerical rule, it will weaken the power of this idea among other Shia and will strengthen elements within Iran itself that are hostile to this principle. Indeed, such a turn of events strikes directly at the hardliners in power in Iran.

Thus, Iran will naturally seek to influence the Iraqi Shiite community, but it will also have to rival it. At least among Arab Shia, the Iraqi Shia are far better positioned to exert influence than is Persian Iran.

Shiite Iraq and Bahrain

Bahrain is virtually a carbon copy of the sectarian balance in Iraq—approximately two-thirds of the Bahraini population is Shia. It is a very old community on the island compared to the more recent arrival a few centuries ago of Sunni Arab tribes who then took over the country under the ruling Al-Khalifa family. The Shia of Bahrain have also been systematically excluded from significant power for a very long time, and have struggled to gain their rights inside the country. The succession to a new Emir, now King, Hamad in Bahrain, brought some promise of reform, but on balance it has been disappointing to the Shia, falling well short of expectations. The Shia are disillusioned and frustrated, and have occasionally resorted to low scale violence in past years, although the violence has largely ceased since the succession of King Hamad.

The Bahraini Shia have already been greatly heartened by the mere possibility now of the emergence of Shiite power in Iraq and are hopeful that Iraq's influence might be able to bring about some change in Bahrain, including even the hope of democratization that would permit the Bahraini Shia to realize the benefits of their demographic weight. A new Iraqi state with strong Shiite voice will unquestionably interest itself in the fate of Shiite brethren in Bahrain and can do so, not on the basis of favoritism for the Shia, but as part of a more general call for democratization.

Shiite Iraq and Saudi Arabia

The potential democratization of the Iraqi political order and the emergence of Shiite dominance in the system has major impact on Saudi Arabia as well, even though the Shia in Saudi Arabia represent only a small minority, perhaps 10 percent of the population. Nonetheless, the Saudi Shia are located in the strategic

[126]

eastern area of the country where the energy sources are found. Furthermore, the Shiite areas of the Kingdom are immediately adjacent to the island of Bahrain, where, as we have seen, the Shia are a majority. Family ties between the two Shiite communities of Saudi Arabia and Bahrain are close and historical. Moreover, while the Shia of Saudi Arabia are only a minority and could not hope to be a major voice in the Kingdom, they are oppressed and bitterly frustrated, the object of not simply discrimination by tradition, but even by de jure laws that limit their participation in society and the free practice of their religion. They have been subject even to *takfir* (denunciation as non-Muslims) by many Wahhabi clerics and their blood declared licit. Anti-Shiism is a foundation stone of hardline Wahhabi thought.

Like the Bahraini Shia, the Shia of Saudi Arabia have been emboldened by the potential rise of Shiite power in Iraq. They nourish hopes that a more powerful voice for Arab Shia in the Gulf will lead to better conditions for them in the Kingdom, and are beginning to ask for equal treatment and conditions as citizens. The Saudi regime is nervous about this shift of power in Iraq, not only for its potential effect on the Kingdom's Shia, but also for the balance of Shia–Sunni power in the Gulf. While the situation is still unclear, there have been many anecdotal reports of growing Wahhabi influence in Iraq, funded by elements within the Saudi and Kuwaiti regimes or society. The question of the role of the Shia in the Kingdom relates directly to the power and legitimacy of the dominant Wahhabi sect which does not countenance any legal religious status for Shia. The Shiite issue will remain a very delicate one in the Kingdom and a subject of great concern to the regime, especially if the Shiite voice in Bahrain should grow and ties between Bahraini and Saudi Shia intensify.

Shiite Iraq and Syria/Lebanon

In sectarian terms, Syria represents almost a reverse image of Iraq. Syria is ruled by a Shiite minority representing some 13 percent of the population, while the majority of the country is Sunni Arab, along with a significant Christian minority. The Shia of Syria are actually 'Alawi, a heterodox form of Shiism that was nevertheless acknowledged by the Islamic Republic of Iran to be a legitimate form of Shiism. Sectarian tensions have abounded in Syria over the past four decades and the Muslim Brotherhood of Syria has engaged in armed violence against the regime periodically, leading to the deaths of many of them and the exile of its leadership, which has been divided along leadership and ideological lines. The Sunni community of Syria is in no way monolithic itself with many divisions, particularly along regional lines. Typically in all countries, sectarian divisions can be intensified and become more monolithic in periods of crisis and instability when sub-national identity gains importance in existential terms. Under any circumstances, the future of Syrian evolution is bound to involve certain instabilities in any transition in power, as the Iraq case demonstrates.

The key question now is the impact of future Shiite power in Iraq and the opening up of Islamist politics there. First, will the return of the Muslim Brotherhood to Iraq open up the prospects for increased support of Iraqi Brotherhood members for any future role in Syria? The Brotherhood remains a banned organization in Syria, but there have been some contacts between the Syrian regime and the more moderate members of the Brotherhood about the possibility of a return to Syria. The Iraqi Brotherhood will undoubtedly have an interest, and now an opportunity and neighboring venue, to become more involved in the future of the Syrian Brotherhood.

[128]

The opposite question pertains to the Shia of Iraq. With newfound power and influence in Iraq, will the Shiite leadership have an interest in supporting close ties with the 'Alawi leadership and its continued domination in Syria? Since 1979, the Iranian regime has maintained an abiding strategic alliance with the Syrian regime that has had much influence in turn upon the Syrian/Iranian influence in Lebanon and especially with the Lebanese Shiite radical organization Hizbollah. Is it possible that, as Shiite Arab power grows in Iraq and influences Iraqi foreign policy, Iraq might begin to replace Iran as the leading role in Syria, especially with the 'Alawi regime and its ties with the Shia of Lebanon who represent a plurality in the country? Will there be an Iranian/Iraqi rivalry for influence in the region and particularly in Syria and Lebanon? The leading Shiite theologian in Lebanon, Sheikh Mohammed Hossein Fadlallah, is a graduate of Najaf and reportedly might be interested in returning to Iraq to play some role there in the future. If so, he would represent a powerful voice in Iraq, and possibly a further counter-balance against Iranian theological leanings. This important question remains open for the future, but suggests a greater role for Iraq in both Syria and Lebanon.

More broadly, all these changes could become part of a general shift within the Arab and Muslim world as regards the role of the Shia that could have major implications for traditional concepts of pan-Arabism and its strong Sunni orientation to date. Indeed, some Sunni nationalist commentators in the Arab world are overtly fearful that this is precisely the "US strategic goal" in bringing about change in Iraq—to tip the sectarian balance against the Sunnis to weaken Arab nationalism and facilitate US domination of the region. In reality such ideas are far more sophisticated – and uncertain in their outcome – that any discussion of American interests in the Middle East ever contains at the policy level. Such paranoia will never die among certain groups and worse, it will be bolstered or "proven" by articles such as this one.

Kurdish Islamism

The Kurds will not be decisive players within the context of Iraqi Islamism. The Kurds have long had their own Islamist movements that have played an important role in supporting Kurdish nationalism. However, Kurdish Islamists in the end have felt they were not able to cooperate with the Brotherhood's Arab members since they believed the Arabs showed insufficient commitment to the special ethnic needs of the Kurds.

The Ansar al-Islam, a radical-jihadi organization with purported "links" with al Qaeda achieved prominence before and after the war against Saddam in 2003. While this radical movement has been located in the mountains of Kurdistan it is not an essentially Kurdish movement.

Despite belief among Islamists that Islam indeed transcends ethnic differences in the name of a broader *umma*, in reality ethnicity often does complicate the achievement of full accord among Islamists of differing ethnic groups when they are contending over local issues. In post-Saddam Iraq, the Kurdish cause thus overrides broader Sunni religious solidarity, at least while the basic elements of the new Iraqi state are being hammered out, including the degree of autonomy which the Kurds will enjoy within the country. It is unlikely then that any sense of Sunni solidarity among the mainly Sunni Kurds with the Arab Sunnis will lead the Kurds to a major commitment against the Shia. Indeed, the Shia may well work to try to meet Kurdish aspirations in order to head off the prospect of any greater Sunni solidarity against the Shia. The chances are that Islamism among the Kurds will retain mainly Kurdish features, at least during this critical period of new national formation inside Iraq.

Conclusion

We can see, then, that political Islam is now in the process of gaining a major role in Iraqi politics in a way that was not possible under Saddam Hussein's Baath regime. It will proceed to affect Iraq and the region in ways that can only be speculated upon here, but over time its influence will be profound in the region, especially if Iraq gradually becomes a model of democratic change and vital sectarian politics.

THE OIL INDUSTRY

5

Iraq in a New Map of Oil Supplies: Implications for Other Gulf Oil Producers

Vera de Ladoucette

Before the Iraq war, the perspective of a regime change in Baghdad had generated concern – or hope, depending on the viewpoint – about an immediate collapse in oil prices. It had been heralded by some as the death sentence for the Organization of Petroleum Exporting Countries (OPEC). It had raised speculations about a dominant role for the American oil industry and had generated illusions concerning a rapid privatization of major oil resources. Not long after the fall of Baghdad, these misconceptions began to fade away, as Iraq's comeback on the oil market has proved to be bumpier than some had expected. However, transitional difficulties should not mislead us. Regime change in Baghdad marks a turning point for the oil sector, be it in Iraq or in other Middle East producing countries. The ineluctable increase in Iraqi oil capacity might affect OPEC cohesion. The expected opening up of the Iraqi oil sector will spur competition for capital. Nevertheless, it is not a purely oil issue, as the time frame is highly dependant on politics.

It is worth considering three issues that are inter-related: the timetable and conditions of Iraq's come back on the oil market; its impact on oil prices; and the mitigating strategies available to other Gulf producers. One could summarize the conclusions as follows:

- Iraq production outlook is to be divided in three phases:
  - Iraq will not reach its pre-March 2003 production level before the end of 2004.
  - Iraq National Oil Company (INOC) will be in charge of building back production capacity to the pre-1990 capacity level. Service companies will be the main beneficiaries of this second phase.
  - The scale and timing of any Iraqi capacity increase beyond 3.5 million barrels per day (mbd) are closely linked to the political situation, as international oil companies (IOCs) have made clear that they will wait for a legitimate Iraqi government to make any long-term commitment. Reaching a production level of 5 mbd by 2010 would require rapid political stabilization.

- Even if it is gradual, Iraq's comeback on the oil market will weigh on prices:
  - In the short term, the downward impact on prices is mitigated by political uncertainties as well as by physical disruptions.
  - In the medium term, the necessity to accommodate Iraq's capacity increase will be a challenge for the cohesion of OPEC, as we expect a limited increase in demand for OPEC oil and competing claims for a higher quota from a few other OPEC producers.

- Competition for capital – and for human resources – will lead other actors to revisit their strategies:

- Some Gulf producers might adopt a pro-active stance and speed up their plans to increase oil production capacity.
- Others are already focusing on gas.
- All will have to consider whether OPEC should go on relinquishing market share to non-OPEC producers.

Assessing the Opportunities

Iraq enjoys the second largest oil reserves in the world, second only to Saudi Arabia (see Figure 5.1).

Figure 5.1
Iraq: Second Reserves in the World

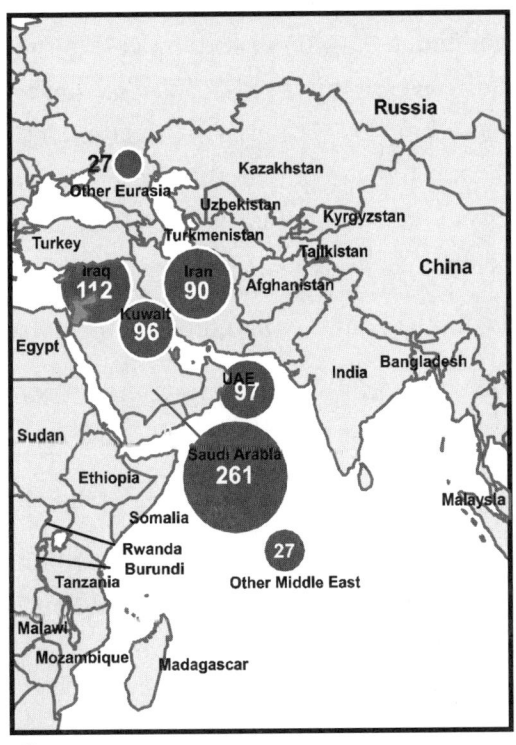

**Oil reserves: Proved (billion barrels)**

Source: Cambridge Energy Research Associates (11917-2C).

However, one should remember that Iraqi reserves are under-estimated, that existing fields are under-developed and that the country is under-explored.

Iraq's proven reserves stand at 112 billion (bn) barrels (13.7% of total OPEC reserves). Ramzi Salman, former Deputy Secretary General of OPEC, who served as Head of Iraq's State and Marketing Organization (SOMO), has recently stressed that the study was done almost 40 years ago, at a time when the factors of recovery, used to calculate the fraction of oil-in-place that is producible, were much smaller than those possible today. Furthermore, of the 526 known oil structures classified as potential prospects, only 125 have been drilled.

Iraq is also an under-developed and under-explored country. Out of 73 already discovered oil fields, only 15 have been put into production. According to Issam Al-Chalabi, the former Iraqi Minister of Oil, Iraq has the potential to produce 4.7 mbd more oil from already discovered fields that are ready to be developed (see Figure 5.2). The main fields are:

- 11 new fields in the south, with a production capacity of 3 mbd;

- 11 fields in the north with a production capacity of about 500,000 bd;

- 3 other fields in central Iraq, with a 300,000 bd capacity.

There is also the possibility to extend the production of existing fields by about 900,000 bd. Moreover, the Western Desert remains largely unexplored, with a promising potential.

Figure 5.2
Iraq Oil Facilities

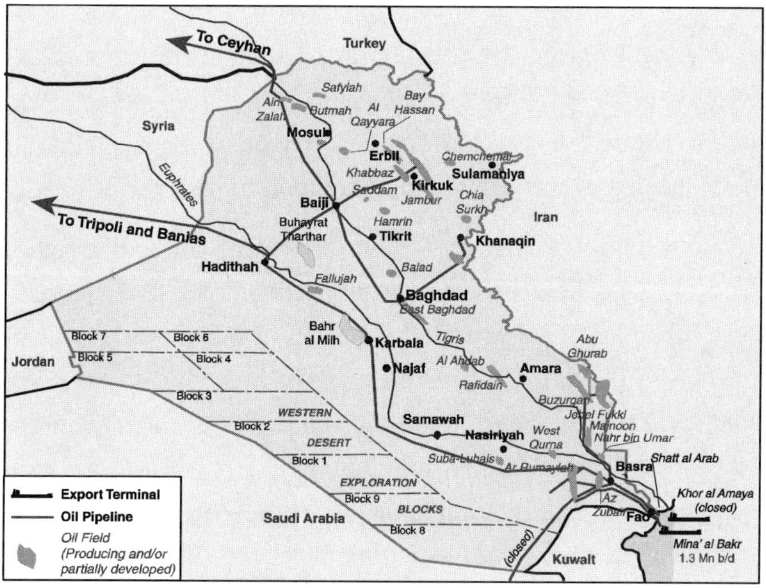

Source: Cambridge Energy Research Associates (30403-2).

To sum up, Iraqi additional reserves can be conservatively estimated at 45 bn barrels, and raising Iraq's production capacity over 6 mbd is not an exploration issue. Three other points play in Iraq's favor:

- Iraqi fields are, for the most part, easy to exploit, with large onshore reservoirs;

- Iraqi oil has a very low cost of production, which is estimated between $1.40 and $1.80 per barrel (depending on the size of the field and the quality of the oil);

- Iraqi oil benefits also from its strategic location, as it can serve both the Asian and the Mediterranean markets.

Calendar and Conditions
for a Slow Build-up of Iraqi Production

A lot was said before the war about the impact of a regime change in Baghdad on the oil sector. At Cambridge Energy Research Associates (CERA) we warned, at the time, against some misconceptions. Recent developments tend to justify our caution.

Illusions about a fast come back of Iraqi oil that would have flooded the market, driving an immediate price collapse, have quickly disappeared. American service companies do lead the restoration of Iraq's production capacity, but American oil companies are not carving up the Iraqi cake, and the first term contracts for lifting Iraqi crude have been awarded as much to European and Asian companies as to American ones. The temptation to have foreigners ruling the Iraqi oil industry, through an Iraqi Oil Advisory Committee, has vanished. Albeit US influence should not be under-estimated, Iraqis are slowly coming back into the driving seat, which means that the ideologically driven suggestion to privatize the upstream sector is starting to fade away. Caution is the name of the game for IOCs, which are not rushing back to Baghdad.

The pace of the recovery, and later on of the build up of Iraq's production capacity, is going to be closely linked to the political calendar.

Restoration to 2.8 mbd Pre-War Capacity Unlikely Before the End of 2004

Far from flooding the market after the fall of Baghdad, Iraqi oil production had barely reached 1 mbd in August 2003, against an average production of 2.5 mbd in the first two months of 2003.

[140]

There was almost no damage due to the war itself, except a direct hit on the K-3 pumping station on the strategic pipeline. However, the slower than expected resumption of Iraqi production as well as exports disruptions are due both to the lack of security and to the difficulties in bringing back power and water facilities.

First, it took time to get the industry started, as the "debaathification" led to a managerial re-organization, while lack of security in the fields discouraged employees to go back to work. Then, looting by some isolated individuals gave way to organized sabotage. After a first series of bombings of oil and gas pipelines in June/July 2003, exports to the Mediterranean, through the Turkish terminal in Ceyhan, which were due to resume on a regular basis by mid-August, had to be postponed by three weeks due to the August 15 and 16 explosions that ruptured the Iraq–Turkey pipeline in two places, several kilometers away (see Figure 5.3).

Figure 5.3
Iraq: A Vulnerable Transportation System

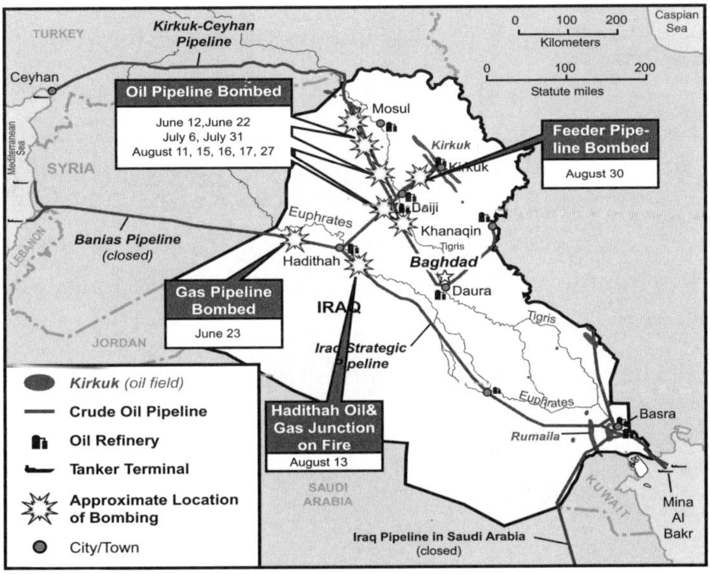

Source: Cambridge Energy Research Associates

Erratic electricity supply has slowed down loadings at the Mina Al Bakr terminal on the Gulf, whereas insufficient filtered-water supplies have delayed much-needed re-injection in some wells, mainly in the south. The looting of the Qarmat Ali water processing plant, which supplies 1.2 mbd of processed water that is utilized for injection in the wells and for the Basrah refinery, has contributed to the slow resumption of production in the south.

The US-sponsored plan – Restoration of Iraqi Oil Infrastructure – which was published on July 24, 2003, was prepared in consultation with the Iraqi Ministry of Oil, the Coalition Provisional Authority (CPA), the US Army Corps of Engineers (USACE) and Kellogg Brown and Root (KBR). Its aim is to restore Iraq production capacity to its 2002 level of 2.8 mbd by April 2004, with a total expenditure of $1.44 billion on 220 projects.

The conditions for achieving this goal on schedule involve a fast US appropriation process for the funds to be available, the absence of any technical problem, good coordination between all parties concerned and the end of sabotage. As long as law and order are not restored in Iraq, it will prove difficult to keep such a tight schedule.

CERA maintains that, under a reasonably optimistic scenario, Iraqi production would increase to 1.8 mbd by December 2003, reach 2.3 mbd in April 2004 and barely reach 2.7 mbd by end 2004 (see Figure 5.4). This schedule is highly dependent on the safety conditions.

Figure 5.4
Iraq's Short-Term Production Outlook

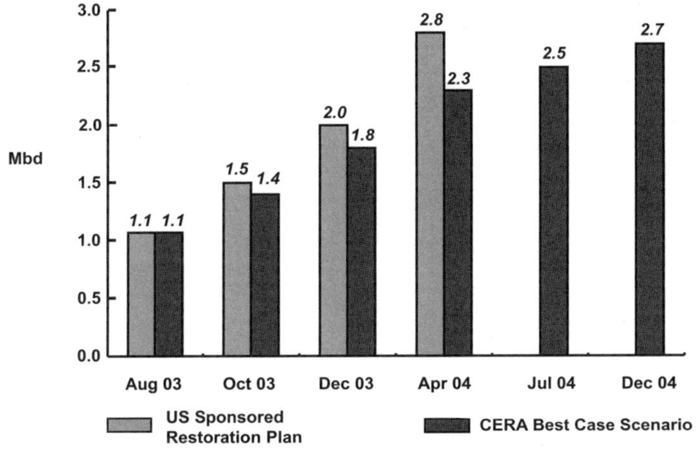

Source: Cambridge Energy Research Associates (30901-1bls).

Build-up to Pre-1990 Capacity by 2007

The first phase is dealing with the rehabilitation of the surface facilities. The second one will focus on restoring the potential of the reservoirs, which have been severely damaged by the policy of maximizing production, regardless of industry best practices, between 1997 and 2002.

Going from 2.7 mbd to the pre-1990 capacity of 3.5 mbd will take at least 3 more years, by rehabilitating existing fields and enhancing their production. Given the 0.1 mbd annual depletion rate, it means adding 1 mbd extra within this time frame and will entail a $5 bn investment.

It is understood that existing fields will remain under the direct responsibility of the Ministry of Oil and will be operated as part of the national reconstruction effort. A large part of the work will be sub-contracted to foreign service-companies.

[143]

Fast Political Stabilization, a Condition to Attain 5 mbd by 2010

Beyond the repair and the rehabilitation of the 11 existing fields, as well as the enhancing of their production to a 3.5 mbd level, Iraq could produce an additional 4 or 5 mbd from the development of existing discoveries.

Given the huge investments required to provide for the basic needs of the population, Iraq will have to turn to IOCs to finance this increase in capacity, but the conditions of the foreign intervention as well as the pace of development are still unclear.

Within CERA, we have been working on a set of scenarios for Iraqi oil, mostly based on different political assumptions. Our base case was, and still is, that Iraq was a highly complex country and that winning the peace would prove more difficult than winning the war.

Oil companies operate on long time-scales—hence their focus on the new rules of investment in Iraq and on the likely durability of these rules. IOCs have made clear that they would be unwilling to commit themselves before the country is fully stabilized and a legitimate Iraqi government is in place. To quote BP's chairman, Lord Browne, at the annual shareholders meeting on April 24, 2003, there will be "no involvement without the support of an Iraqi government recognized by the world community and the Iraqi people." All the other major oil companies, on both sides of the Atlantic, have adopted the same stance. For the time being, IOCs have a wait and see attitude; they are trying to build or revive networks and to show goodwill.

Should elections take place by the end of 2004, time will be needed to adopt a Hydrocarbons law, decide on a fiscal regime and agree on contractual terms (see Figure 5.5).

Figure 5.5
Iraq: 5 mbd by 2010?

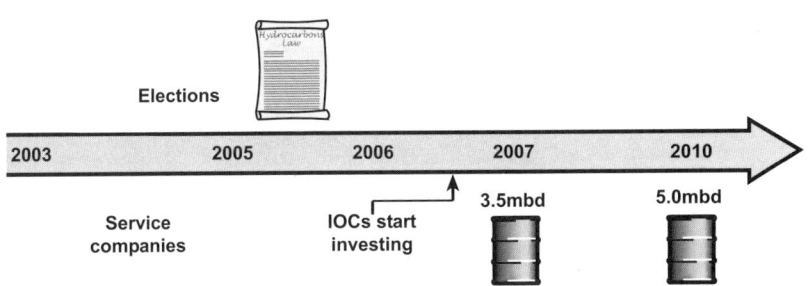

Source: Cambridge Energy Research Associates (30301-55).

It is expected that the development of new fields will be implemented by consortia, led by major international companies. These consortia might involve some of the companies that had signed or negotiated agreements or understandings prior to the war, once the legal claims and political hurdles are cleared.

No decision has yet been made on the type of contracts. A provision stating that oil in the ground is the sole property of the Iraqi people is likely to be included in each contract. Modified buy-back contracts might be awarded for undeveloped fields, but production sharing contracts (PSC) as well as development and production contracts (DPC) that have formed the basis of discussions with international oil companies since June 2000 might also be considered. Risk contracts might be available for exploration concessions.

Iraq might present an opportunity for emerging major companies, because the IOCs are not better established than themselves. These large independent companies would prefer INOC to adopt the Norwegian model, in which opportunities are made available for tender, with state participation, but will be also willing to join a consortium of IOCs.

[145]

Whereas for the first phase, the prerequisite is restoring law and order, political stabilization is essential for this third phase. Major investments by IOCs are unlikely to start before 2006/2007. Reaching a production capacity of 5 mbd could still prove to be an ambitious target.

Iraq: A Key to Oil Prices for the Years to Come

Iraq will be a determining factor of price trends in the coming years. In 2003, Iraq crude production averaged 1.25 mbd. It might add 1.2 mbd in 2004. Additional supplies could then increase by up to 2.5 mbd by 2010.

However, Iraq is not and will not be the only key to oil prices. Without entering into details, it is worth recalling a few other issues:

- Iraq is not the only major oil producer, and we have seen recently how events in Venezuela or Nigeria could impact on oil prices. Disruptions in any major producing country, be it an OPEC member or not, have an immediate impact on price.

- Non-OPEC production growth (and OPEC/non-OPEC relations) is another major factor.

- Prices are not only a matter of supply, but also a matter of demand. The picture is not the same when demand is almost flat, as in 1998 and 2002 (+0.3 mbd), or grows by about 2 mbd, as in 1996 and 1997.

Short-Term Price Outlook

The short-term price outlook is highly dependent on the course of Iraqi production over the months to come. However, the situation in Venezuela and Nigeria will need to be closely monitored.

[146]

In the "Iraq comes back scenario," expectations were that prices would stay firm in the fourth quarter of 2003, because of low inventories and possible temporary supply disruptions (see Figure 5.6). Prices would then ease gradually in 2004, as the average for Brent would slip from $28 in the first quarter to $ 23.50 in the third quarter, with a yearly average over $25.

Figure 5.6
2000-2004 Oil Price Environment: Brent

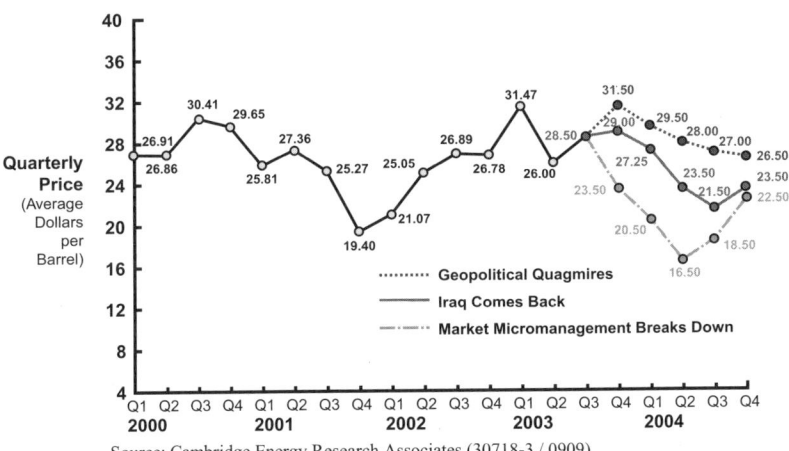

Source: Cambridge Energy Research Associates (30718-3 / 0909).

A Challenge for OPEC

The issue is not whether a new Iraqi regime decides to leave OPEC, or even whether Iraq will abide by a quota. It is a simple matter of numbers. It is not in the other OPEC members' interest to have Iraq leave the Organization, as Baghdad would not then be bound by any constraint. It might be in Iraq's best interest to stay within OPEC, inasmuch as preserving the cohesion of the Organization might help fight a downward price trend.

Given CERA's assessment of non-OPEC oil production (fast growth till 2007, slowing gradually up to 2010), there is not much room for OPEC production to grow until 2007 (about 1.5 mbd). However, the situation should improve in the latter part of the decade, as non-OPEC production growth slows down. Even if Iraq's comeback on the oil market is sluggish, and if Baghdad doesn't reach its 3.5 mbd pre-1990 capacity before 2007, Iraqi oil will eat up any demand increase for OPEC in the years to come.

How OPEC will accommodate Iraq is a real issue, as it comes at a time when other OPEC members want the whole quota system to be revisited to take into account production capacity increases. Algeria and Nigeria have already asked for a higher quota; Libya is starting to push its case. Apparently the UAE is also preparing the ground, as the Middle East Economic Survey (MEES) has published that plans were under way to bring capacity from the current 2.6 mbd level to 3.6 mbd by 2006.

Last time Iraq had a quota, it was at parity with Iran. This was part of the deal achieved at the end of the 1981–1988 Iraq–Iran war.

Some major OPEC members say that parity with Iran is now history, but it will be difficult to ignore. To pre-empt any argument over the fact that Iraq's reserves (112 bn barrels) were higher than Iran's (90 bn barrels), Tehran announced in July 2003 some major discoveries, hereby revising its reserves up to 131 bn barrels.

Iran's quota stands today over 3.729 mbd. It is a distant goal for Iraq, but the real quota issue is not only how many barrels each country has, but what is the size of each producer within OPEC.

In 1990, both Iraq and Iran had 14.26 percent of OPEC 11 ceiling.[1] A simple look at the break out of today's distribution of quotas for OPEC 10 (excluding Iraq) between 10 members shows what a daunting challenge OPEC is facing.

For the sake of the argument, Table 5.1 shows what would be the quota of each member within a notional production ceiling of 27 mbd in 2006. Is Saudi Arabia ready to go down from current 8.25 mbd to 6.6 mbd? Could the UAE and Kuwait accept to go below 2 mbd? Is it realistic to show Indonesia over 1.6 mbd?

Table 5.1
Quotas Nightmare

OPEC pre Gulf war quotas assuming 27 mbd by 2005			Current distribution for OPEC10			A Notional 27 mbd ceiling with the 1990 distribution	
1990			2003				
	%			%			
	7/90 OPEC11	7/90 OPEC11		6/03 quota	OPEC10		
Algeria	0.827	3.76	Algeria	0.811	3.19	Algeria	1.01
Indonesia	1.374	6.24	Indonesia	1.317	5.19	Indonesia	1.68
Iran	3.140	14.26	Iran	3.729	14.68	Iran	3.85
Kuwait	1.500	6.81	Kuwait	2.038	8.02	Kuwait	1.84
Libya	1.233	5.60	Libya	1.36	5.35	Libya	1.51
Nigeria	1.611	7.32	Nigeria	2.092	8.24	Nigeria	1.98
Qatar	0.371	1.68	Qatar	0.658	2.59	Qatar	0.45
UAE	1.500	6.81	UAE	2.217	8.73	UAE	1.84
Saudi Arabia	5.380	24.43	Saudi Arabia	8.256	32.50	Saudi Arabia	6.60
Venezuela	1.945	8.83	Venezuela	2.923	11.51	Venezuela	2.38
			OPEC 10	25.4	100.00		
Iraq	3.140	14.26	Iraq			Iraq	3.85
Total OPEC13						Total OPEC11	27.00
Total OPEC11*	22.02	100.00					

* Without Ecuador and Gabon who left OPEC respectively on January 1993 and January 1995.

Source: Cambridge Energy Research Associates.

The next step follows logically. Iraq's return might force some OPEC members to wonder whether the Organization should go on losing market share to non-OPEC producers, as has been the case for the last five years (see Figure 5.7), hoping for a turn-around that might happen after 2007.

Figure 5.7
OPEC Share of Total Suppliers

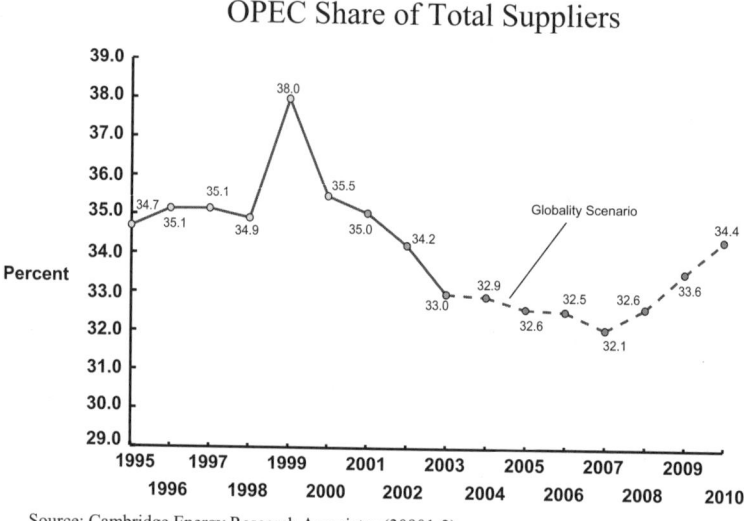

Source: Cambridge Energy Research Associates (30901-2).

Revisiting Upstream Strategies

Iraq should not be looked at in a vacuum. It should not be considered only from the countries' viewpoint, but also from the oil companies' perspective.

Other countries are integrating Iraq's come back in their thinking, be it because of the price impact, as we have seen concerning OPEC, or because the amount of capital as well as the pool of human resources available for the oil industry are not unlimited. It is an interactive situation. Changes in the investment climate are anticipated in the Middle East, but also in Russia and the Caspian.

Once oil companies will be able to invest in Iraq, they will judge the opportunities by the same criteria as they use for other investments, namely rate of return, growth potential, and ability to book the reserves according to the Securities and Exchange Commission (SEC) criteria.

A few recent moves are not a matter of coincidence. It shows that other Gulf producers are starting to take into account Iraq's expected opening up of the oil sector.

Speeding-up Production Capacity Increases

UAE to Increase Capacity by 2006

As has already been mentioned, the UAE has let know that it intended to increase capacity to 3.58 mbd by 2006. This growth will come from Abu Dhabi and hinges mainly on the timing of an agreement with IOCs on the expansion of the offshore Upper Zakum field from 0.55 mbd to 1.2 mbd. Currently, the Zakum Development Company (ZADCO) is owned by ADNOC (88 percent) and Japan Offshore Development Company (JODCO) for the remaining 12 percent. The principle of awarding 28 percent of ZADCO to one or several IOCs has been decided. Short-listed companies made technical presentations in April 2002, but the Supreme Petroleum Council has still to announce its decision. Abu Dhabi Company for Onshore Oil Operations (ADCO) should also contribute by about 0.3 mbd to the UAE capacity increase.

A Revival of Project Kuwait

After a long parliamentary battle that has paralyzed Project Kuwait since its inception in 1998, the Kuwaiti government has seized the opportunity of a seemingly friendlier Parliament, after the July 5, 2003 elections, to revive its project to further open up upstream to foreign companies.

On August 5, the Supreme Petroleum Council (SPC) approved the composition of three consortia formed to bid for the expansion of the northern fields from current 600,000 bd to 900,000 bd.

Kuwait Petroleum Company (KPC) is arguing that Operating Service Agreements (OSA) can be signed with foreign companies without infringing on the sovereignty of the state or oil ownership, and that this would not require specific legislation, but could be covered by a blanket legislation allowing foreign firms to operate in the country in this way.

Many deputies object to the principle of foreign companies being awarded 20/30-year contracts, some worry about the transparency of these agreements, and a few still insist on having the Parliament approve by law each and every oil contract. It remains to be seen whether the government will be able to convince legislators in the National Assembly that foreign intervention is the key to expanding Kuwait's production capacity and that Project Kuwait is only an indispensable first step to the doubling of Kuwait's capacity to 5 mbd by 2020.

Attracting Foreign Capital in the Gas Sector

There is no pre-determined share for oil development versus gas in IOCs allocation of capital, and Iraq's expected opening is also a matter of concern for countries that focus on gas.

A New Step Forward for Qatar LNG

Qatar has been for a long time at the forefront of the liquefied natural gas (LNG) expansion in the Middle East. Doha might be more attentive to Tehran's plans to develop its share of the giant North Dome field (South Pars on the Iranian side of the border) than to Iraq's opening of the oil sector. However, it cannot ignore that in a few years competition for capital might be fiercer.

Qatar plans to attract $25 bn in investments in order to increase LNG's exports capacity from the current 18.8 billion cubic meters per year (bcm/y) to 83 bcm/y by 2010. ExxonMobil's project to export 20 bcm/y to the United Kingdom and the rest of Europe would be a major step in that direction, but achieving this goal depends also on the outcome of current discussions about supplying LNG to the United States. Should Qatar be able to reach its ambitious target of 83 bcm by 2010, it would almost certainly overtake Malaysia, Algeria and Indonesia to become the world's largest LNG exporter. Allocation of sufficient capital toward the new projects is clearly one of several conditions if this goal is to be achieved.

Go-Ahead for Foreign Investment in Saudi Gas Sector

On June 5, when ExxonMobil, the leader of Core Venture 1, received a letter "confirming the termination of the Preparatory Agreement," many thought that this decision was putting the last nail in the coffin of foreign investment in the Saudi gas sector.

The "Gas Initiative" might be dead, as it was initially envisaged – a multibillion dollars ambitious plan, with both an upstream and a strong downstream component – but the Saudi government has made clear that foreign investments in the gas sector were indeed welcomed and that it intended to speed up the process.

Barely a few weeks later, two of the IOCs that had been negotiating Core Venture 3 (Shell and Total) came to an agreement with Saudi Aramco on the development of the upstream part of Core Venture 3.

Furthermore, the Saudi Ministry of Oil invited 41 international companies in London on July 22/23, 2003 to learn about the details of a new plan to open up the gas sector, by offering for natural gas exploration and production the area that was initially included in Core Venture 3.

The 120,000 km acreage is divided in three contract areas, and there is no more talk about coupling upstream with power generation, desalination or petrochemicals. However, it still remains to be seen whether the main hurdle (coming to an agreement about a rate of return that is acceptable by both parties) can be overcome.

Conclusion

For months now, the world has kept its eyes on Iraq. People debated about the urgency of fighting a war to bring regime change. Later, they hoped that the battle would be short and with as low casualties as possible. After the fall of Baghdad, one wondered about the way Iraqis might take their destiny in their hands. Soon, concerns rose about escalating violence. Re-establishing law and order became the priority for every party involved.

One can only hope that Iraq will leave front-page news as soon as possible. However, for the oil industry it will remain a focal point for the years to come. The size and the timing of Iraqi oil expansion will affect neighboring countries as well as oil companies, and might even impact the world economy.

CONTRIBUTORS

PATRICK CLAWSON is Deputy Director of the Washington Institute for Near East Policy. He is a co-author of the Institute's recent publication *Winning the Peace in the Middle East: A Bipartisan Blueprint for Postwar U.S. Policy*, which has been endorsed by a group of eminent Americans. His other recent works as editor, author or co-author include: *How to Build a New Iraq after Saddam* (The Washington Institute, 2003); *Iran Under Khatami: A Political, Economic, and Military Assessment* (The Washington Institute, 1998); *Iraq Strategy Review: Options for U.S. Policy* (The Washington Institute, 1998); *U.S. Sanctions on Iran* (The Emirates Center for Strategic Studies and Research, 1997); *Energy Security in the Twenty-First Century* (NDU Press, 1995); and *Iran's Strategic Intentions and Capabilities*, editor (NDU Press, 1994). He is the author of more than thirty articles on the Middle East in *Foreign Affairs, Iranian Studies, International Economy, Middle East Journal* and other academic journals. Dr. Clawson has also written opinion/editorial articles in the *New York Times, Wall Street Journal* and *Washington Post*, among other newspapers. Dr. Clawson is senior editor of the *Middle East Quarterly*. He has testified more than a dozen times before congressional committees.

From 1993 to 1997, Dr. Clawson was a senior research professor at the Institute for National Strategic Studies of the National Defense University in Washington, DC, where he was the editor of the Institute's flagship annual publication, *Strategic Assessment*. From 1981 to 1992, he was a research economist for four years each at the International Monetary Fund, the World Bank and the Foreign Policy Research Institute, where he was also editor of *Orbis*, a quarterly review of foreign affairs. His doctoral degree is from the New School for Social Research and his bachelor's degree from Oberlin College, both in economics. He speaks Persian (Farsi), French, Spanish, German and Hebrew.

BATHSHEBA N. CROCKER is a 2002–2003 International Affairs Fellow for the Council on Foreign Relations. She is based at the Center for Strategic and International Studies (CSIS) in Washington, DC, where she is working with CSIS's Post-Conflict Reconstruction Project. She has co-authored three recent CSIS reports on post-conflict reconstruction in Iraq – *Winning the Peace: An Action Strategy for a Post-Conflict Iraq; Postwar Iraq: Are We Ready;* and *Iraq's Post-Conflict Reconstruction: Field Review and Recommendations.* She was also a member of a CSIS-led reconstruction assessment team that went to Iraq in July 2003 at the request of the US Department of Defense. Dr. Crocker co-authored "Winning the Peace in Iraq," which appeared in the Spring 2003 edition of *The Washington Quarterly*, and has written chapters on post-conflict reconstruction in Kosovo, Iraq and Sierra Leone.

Dr. Crocker appears regularly as a commentator on major news programs, including CNN, BBC and NPR. Dr. Crocker most recently worked as an attorney-adviser in the Legal Adviser's Office at the US Department of State, where she focused on foreign assistance and appropriations law issues. Prior to that, she served as the Deputy US Special Representative for the Southeast Europe Initiative in Rome, Italy. She has previously served as the executive assistant to the Deputy National Security Advisor at the White House, and as an attorney-adviser at the State Department, working on issues related to economic sanctions. Dr. Crocker received a Bachelor of Arts from Stanford University, a Doctor of

Jurisprudence (JD) from Harvard Law School and a Masters in Law and Diplomacy from the Fletcher School at Tufts University.

KENNETH KATZMAN, a specialist with the Congressional Research Service since 1991, serves as a senior Middle East analyst for the US Congress. His areas of specialization include Iran, Iraq, the Gulf states, Afghanistan and terrorist groups operating in the Middle East and South Asia. He provides reports and briefings to members of Congress and their staff on US policy and legislation on these areas.

Dr. Katzman was assigned to the House International Relations Committee during 1996 and from July 2001 to March 2002 to work on Middle Eastern issues. During 1998, he wrote working papers on the ballistic missile capabilities of Iran and Iraq for the Commission to Assess the Ballistic Missile Threat to the United States, better known as the Rumsfeld Commission. In late 1999, the Atlantic Council published his study, *U.S.-Iran Relations: An Analytic Compendium of U.S. Policies, Laws, and Regulations*.

From 1989 to 1991, Dr. Katzman was an analyst at Defense Systems Inc., where he produced extensive analyses for clients in the defense and intelligence community. From 1985 to 1989, he worked at the Central Intelligence Agency, where he was responsible for writing reports for US Middle East policymakers on leadership dynamics in Iran, Iraq and the Gulf states.

Dr. Katzman has written numerous articles in various publications, including the *Middle East Quarterly*, *Middle East Insight* and *Caspian Crossroads*. He is the author of *The Warriors of Islam: Iran's Revolutionary Guard* (1993), and contributed a chapter on "The Gulf Cooperation Council: Prospects for Collective Security" in M.E. Ahrari and J.H. Noyes (eds) *The Persian Gulf After the Cold War* (1993). Dr. Katzman has given many presentations and briefings, and has traveled widely to Central Asia, the Caucasus, Asia, the Middle East and the Gulf for official discussions on topics in his area of responsibility.

Dr. Katzman received his Ph.D. in Political Science from New York University in 1991. The topic of his dissertation was "Iran's Islamic Revolutionary Guard Corps: Radical Ideology Despite Institutionalization in the Islamic Republic."

GRAHAM E. FULLER was until recently a resident senior political consultant at RAND Corporation in Washington, DC, and is a former Vice Chairman of the National Intelligence Council at the CIA. He served twenty years in the Foreign Service, mostly in the Muslim world, working in Germany, Turkey, Lebanon, Saudi Arabia, North Yemen, Afghanistan and Hong Kong.

In 1982, Mr. Fuller was appointed the National Intelligence Officer for Near East and South Asia at the CIA. In 1986, he became Vice Chairman of the National Intelligence Council, also at the CIA, with overall responsibility for all national level strategic forecasting. In 1988, he left the government and joined the RAND Corporation where his work was primarily on the Middle East, Central Asia, South and Southeast Asia, and ethnic problems of the former Soviet Union.

His work for RAND included a 1991 study on the geopolitical implications of the Palestinian *intifada*; a series of studies on Islamic fundamentalism in Turkey, Sudan, Afghanistan, Pakistan and Algeria; the survivability of Iraq; the new geopolitics of Central Asia after the fall of the USSR; and problems of democratization and Islam. He is author of several articles and books, among which are *The Future of Political Islam* (2003); *The Arab Shi'a: The Forgotten Muslims* (1999; with Rend Francke); *Turkey's Kurdish*

Question (1997; with Henry Barkey); *A Sense of Siege: The Geopolitics of Islam and the West* (1994; with Ian Lesser). Mr. Fuller is a regular opinion/editorial contributor to the *New York Times, Washington Post, Los Angeles Times* and *Christian Science Monitor.* He has appeared frequently on ABC's "Nightline," ABC Evening News, CNN, PBS Newshour with Jim Lehrer, and Fox Television News. He also comments regularly for BBC Radio, Voice of America and other news stations. He has an extensive knowledge of foreign languages including Russian, Turkish, Arabic and Chinese, and is the author of the popular book *How to Learn a Foreign Language.*

Mr. Fuller received his BA and MA in Russian and Middle Eastern Studies at Harvard University.

VERA DE LADOUCETTE is Senior Director of Middle East Research and Head of the Europe and Asia Gas and Power Team at Cambridge Energy Research Associates (CERA) in Paris, France. Ms. De Ladoucette is a distinguished expert in international relations and the energy industry, and has held posts in both government and industry. Before joining CERA, Ms. De Ladoucette was Senior Vice President for International Relations at TotalFinaElf, where she was responsible for government relations, country assessment and OPEC. Until the merger between TotalFina and Elf in 2000, she held a similar position at Elf Aquitaine (1993–2000) as Vice President, International Relations. Ms. De Ladoucette joined Elf Aquitaine as Deputy Director for International Affairs in 1982, before being appointed Special Adviser to the Executive Vice President for Refining, Marketing and Trading (1989–1993). Previously, she had been an advisor for International Affairs to the Undersecretary for Energy at the Ministry of Industry in France (1975–1982).

In January 2000, Ms. De Ladoucette was appointed as *Chevalier de la Legion d'Honneur* by the French government for her contribution to the field of energy. She is a Member of the Board of the International Center for Research on Women. Ms. De Ladoucette is a graduate of the Institute d'Études Politiques in Paris and holds a Master's Degree in Law and a Bachelor's Degree in Sociology.

Chapter 1

1. Office of the Secretary-General, United Nations, "Report of the Secretary-General on the United Nations Interim Administration Mission in Kosovo," January 29, 2003.

2. Carl Bildt, *Peace Journey: The Struggle for Peace in Bosnia* (London: Weidenfeld and Nicolson, 1998), 390.

3. Zogby International, "The First Scientific Poll of Current Iraqi Public Opinion," *The American Enterprise*, August 2003; Richard Burkholder, "Ousting Saddam Hussein 'Was Worth Hardships Endured Since Invasion,' Say Citizens of Baghdad," The Gallup Organization, September 24, 2003.

4. Agence France Press, "Arab States Welcome Iraqi Council Despite Unease Over Occupation," July 15, 2003.

5. "Arab Human Development Report 2002," United Nations Development Programme, at <www.org/rbas/ahdr/english2002.html>

6. Reuel Marc Gerecht, "Be Careful What You Wish For," *On the Issues*, American Enterprise Institute, September 2003, 3.

7. Martin Indyk, "Back to the Bazaar," *Foreign Affairs* (January/ February 2002): 80–81.

8. Reform petition delivered to Crown Prince Abdullah on September 24, 2003, entitled "In Defense of the Nation," at <www.ccc.nps.navy. mil/rsepResources.si/oct03/abdullahletter9-24.pdf>

Chapter 2

1. That agenda has been described by Iraqis as a plot to dominate the Middle East, exploit and embezzle Iraq's oil, and defend Israeli interests. *Governing Iraq*, International Crisis Group (ICG) Middle East Report No. 17 (August 25, 2003), 4.

2. "Iraq's Post-Conflict Reconstruction: A Field Review and Recommendations," Center for Strategic and International Studies (CSIS) report, July 17, 2003, 1, at <http://www.csis.org.>

3. "Remarks by Secretary of Defense Donald H. Rumsfeld," Council on Foreign Relations, New York, May 27, 2003.

4. Yitzhak Nakash, "The Shi'ites and the Future of Iraq," *Foreign Affairs* 82:4 (July/August 2003): 25.

5. President George W. Bush, "Address to the Nation," Washington, DC, September 7, 2003, at <http://www.whitehouse.gov/news/releases/2003/09/print/20030907-1.html>

6. "Remarks by Secretary Rumsfeld," Council on Foreign Relations, op. cit.

7. See Colin L. Powell, "Remarks at the Elliot School of International Affairs," George Washington University, Washington, DC, September 5, 2003.

8. Paul Wolfowitz, "Prepared Statement," Senate Armed Services Committee, September 9, 2003.

9. "Governing Iraq," op. cit., ii.

10. Mark Fineman, Warran Vieth and Robin Wright, "In an Iraq Without an Army, Perils Abound," *Los Angeles Times*, August 24, 2003.

11. Ibid.

12. Sadly, one member of the Governing Council itself – Akila Hashimi, one of the Council's three women – was shot and killed in Baghdad in late September 2003, allegedly by Baath Party loyalists.

13. Rory McCarthy, *Guardian*, September 1, 2003.

14. Tarel Al-Issawi, "Governing Council Member Demands End to U.S. Occupation at Brother's Funeral in Najaf," Associated Press, September 2, 2003.

15. Dexter Filkins, "For a Bleak Horizon, Rose Tinted Glass," *New York Times*, September 7, 2003.

16. Dexter Filkins, "U.S. and the Iraqis Discuss Creating Bog Militia Force," *New York Times*, August 31, 2003, A1.

17. Ibid.

18. Neil MacFarquhar, "Rising Tide of Islamic Militants See Iraq as Ultimate Battlefield," *New York Times*, August 13, 2003, A1.

19. Peter Finn and Susan Schmidt, "Al Qaeda Plans a Front in Iraq," *Washington Post*, September 7, 2003, A1.

20. Jessica Stern, "How America Created a Terrorist Haven," *New York Times*, August 20, 2003, A21.

21. L. Paul Bremer III, "Iraq's Path to Sovereignty," *Washington Post*, September 8, 2003, A21.

22. Gareth Evans, "Only Self-Rule Will Bring Stability to Iraq," *Financial Times*, August 26, 2003, 17

23. "Governing Iraq," op. cit., 17.

24. Dexter Filkins and Neil MacFarquhar, "U.S. Official Tells Iraqis to Assert More Authority," *New York Times*, August 21, 2003, A12.

25. Fouad Ajami, "Iraq and the Arabs' Future," *Foreign Affairs* 82:1(January/February 2003): 5.

26. Ibid.

27. Ibid.

28. "Rumsfeld Plays Down Shiite Influence," *Baltimore Sun*, April 26, 2003, A9. Secretary of State Colin Powell has recognized that Muslims could play a role in Iraq's new government so long as they embrace democracy. Ibid.

29. Barry Schweid, "Rumsfeld Rules Out Religious Iraqi Government," Associated Press Online, April 25, 2003. Similarly, President Bush has stated, "One thing is certain: We will not impose a government on Iraq. We will help that nation build a government of, by and for the Iraqi people." Ibid.

30. Nakash, op. cit., 24–25.

31. Daniel Byman, "After the Storm: U.S. Policy Toward Iraq Since 1991," *Political Science Quarterly*, 115:4 (Winter 2000/2001): 498

32. Ajami, op. cit., 12.

33. "Iraq's Shiites Under Occupation," International Crisis Group Middle East Briefing (September 9, 2003), 3.

34. Nakash, op. cit., 24.

35. "Governing Iraq," op. cit., 12.

36. "Iraq's Shiites Under Occupation," op. cit., 2.

37. David Ignatius, "Letting Iraq Save Itself," *Washington Post*, September 5, 2003, A21.

38. "Governing Iraq," op. cit., 14.

39. "Iraq's Shiites Under Occupation," op. cit., 21.

40. "Governing Iraq," op. cit., 16–17

41. Saddam allegedly cut off power when he wanted to "punish" Iraqis.

42. Peter Slevin and Vernon Loeb, "Bremer: Iraq Effort to Cost Tens of Billions," *Washington Post*, August 27, 2003, A1.

43. James Harding, "Bush Picks Fundraiser to Revive Iraqi Business," *Financial Times*, August 8, 2003, 9.

44. See Neil King Jr., "Bush Officials Draft Broad Plan for Free-Market Economy in Iraq," *Wall Street Journal*, May 1, 2003.

45. John B. Taylor, Under-Secretary for International Affairs, Department of the Treasury, Testimony, Senate Foreign Relations Committee, June 4, 2003.

46. Ibid.

47. "A Wiser Peace: An Action Strategy for a Post-Conflict Iraq," CSIS Report, January 2003, 23, at <http://www.csis.org.>

48. Michael Monderer and David Mulford, "Iraqi Debt, Like War, Divides the West," *Financial Times*, June 23, 2003, 19.

49. "Governing Iraq," op. cit., 4.

50. S/Res/1483, May 22, 2003, 12–14, 20.

51. Warren Vieth, "U.S. to Let Iraq Manage Its Oil," *Los Angeles Times*, August 18, 2003, 1.

52. Edmund Sanders and Chris Kraul, "Bombing Disrupts Flow of Oil," *Los Angeles Times*, August 17, 2003, 3.

53. John Tierney, "A Popular Idea: Give Oil Money to the People Rather Than the Despots," *New York Times*, September 10, 2003.

54. W. Andrew Terrill, "Nationalism, Sectarianism, and the Future of the U.S. Presence in Post-Saddam Iraq," Strategic Studies Institute monograph 37 (July 2003).

55. Ibid.

Chapter 3

1. "The Iraqi National Congress and the International Community," Document provided by INC representatives, February 1993.

2. C.J. Chivers, "Repulsing Attack by Islamic Militants: Iraqi Kurds Tell of Atrocities," *New York Times*, December 6, 2002.

3. "US Uncertain About Northern Iraq Group's Link to Al Qaida," *Dow Jones Newswire*, March 18, 2002.

4. An account of this shift in US strategy is essayed in Jim Hoagland, "How CIA's Secret War on Saddam Collapsed," *Washington Post*, June 26, 1997.

5. Iraq Liberation Act (ILA, HR 4655, PL 105-338).

6. One account of Bush Administration internal debates on the strategy is found in Seymour Hersh, "The Debate Within," *The New Yorker*, March 11, 2002.

7. "Bremer Reviews Progress, Plans for Iraq Reconstruction," *Washington File* (Transcript), June 23, 2003.

8. Anthony Shadid, "Iraqi Clerics Unite in Rare Alliance," *Washington Post*, August 17, 2003.

9. "White House Notes Successful Results of Iraq Liberation," August 8, 2003, at <http://www.usinfo.state.gov/xarchives>

Chapter 4

1. Syed Saleem Shahzad, "A Third Force Awaits US in Iraq," *Asia Times*, March 1, 2003.

2. Ibid.

3. Bassim Al Azami, "The Muslim Brotherhood: Genesis and Development," in Faleh Abdul-Jabar (ed.) *Ayatollahs, Sufis, and Ideologues* (London: Saqi Books, 2002).

Chapter 5

1. In order to ease the comparison, the production of two countries that have subsequently left OPEC, Gabon and Ecuador, have been taken out of the initial 22.49 mbd ceiling.

BIBLIOGRAPHY

"A Wiser Peace: An Action Strategy for a Post-Conflict Iraq." CSIS Report, January 2003, at <http://www.csis.org.>

"Arab Human Development Report 2002." United Nations Development Programme, at <www.org/rbas/ahdr/english2002.html>

"Arab States Welcome Iraqi Council Despite Unease Over Occupation." Agence France Press, July 15, 2003.

"Bremer Reviews Progress, Plans for Iraq Reconstruction." Washington File (Transcript), *June 23, 2003.*

"Governing Iraq." International Crisis Group Middle East Report No. 17 (August 25, 2003).

"In Defense of the Nation." Reform petition delivered to Crown Prince Abdullah on September 24, 2003, at <www.ccc.nps.navy.mil/rsepResources.si/oct03/abdullahletter9-24.pdf>

"Iraq's Post-Conflict Reconstruction: A Field Review and Recommendations." Center for Strategic and International Studies (CSIS) Report, July 17, 2003. <http://www.csis.org.>

"Iraq's Shiites Under Occupation." International Crisis Group Middle East Briefing (September 9, 2003).

"Remarks by Secretary of Defense Donald H. Rumsfeld." Council on Foreign Relations, New York, May 27, 2003.

"Report of the Secretary-General on the United Nations Interim Administration Mission in Kosovo." Office of the Secretary-General, United Nations, January 29, 2003.

"Rumsfeld Plays Down Shiite Influence." *Baltimore Sun*, April 26, 2003.

"The Iraqi National Congress and the International Community." *Iraqi National Congress,* February 1993.

[169]

"US Uncertain About Northern Iraq Group's Link to Al Qaida." Dow Jones Newswire, March 18, 2002.

"White House Notes Successful Results of Iraq Liberation." August 8, 2003, at <http://www.usinfo.state.gov/xarchives>

Ajami, Fouad. "Iraq and the Arabs' Future." *Foreign Affairs* 82:1(January/ February 2003).

Al Azami, Bassim. "The Muslim Brotherhood: Genesis and Development." In Faleh Abdul-Jabar (ed.) *Ayatollahs, Sufis, and Ideologues* (London: Saqi Books, 2002).

Al-Issawi, Tarel. "Governing Council Member Demands End to U.S. Occupation at Brother's Funeral in Najaf." Associated Press, September 2, 2003.

Bildt, Carl. *Peace Journey: The Struggle for Peace in Bosnia* (London: Weidenfeld and Nicolson, 1998).

Bremer III, L. Paul. "Iraq's Path to Sovereignty." *Washington Post*, September 8, 2003.

Burkholder, Richard. "Ousting Saddam Hussein 'Was Worth Hardships Endured Since Invasion,' Say Citizens of Baghdad." The Gallup Organization, September 24, 2003.

Byman, Daniel. "After the Storm: U.S. Policy Toward Iraq Since 1991." *Political Science Quarterly* 115: 4 (Winter 2000/2001).

Chivers, C.J. "Repulsing Attack by Islamic Militants: Iraqi Kurds Tell of Atrocities." *New York Times*, December 6, 2002.

Evans, Gareth. "Only Self-Rule Will Bring Stability to Iraq." *Financial Times*, August 26, 2003.

Filkins, Dexter and Neil MacFarquhar. "U.S. Official Tells Iraqis to Assert More Authority." *New York Times*, August 21, 2003.

Filkins, Dexter. "For a Bleak Horizon, Rose Tinted Glass." *New York Times*, September 7, 2003.

Filkins, Dexter. "U.S. and the Iraqis Discuss Creating Bog Militia Force." *New York Times*, August 31, 2003.

Fineman, Mark, Warran Vieth and Robin Wright. "In an Iraq Without an Army, Perils Abound." *Los Angeles Times*, August 24, 2003.

Finn, Peter and Susan Schmidt. "Al Qaeda Plans a Front in Iraq." *Washington Post*, September 7, 2003.

Gerecht, Reuel Marc. "Be Careful What You Wish For." *On the Issues.* American Enterprise Institute, September 2003.

Harding, James. "Bush Picks Fundraiser to Revive Iraqi Business." *Financial Times*, August 8, 2003.

Hersh, Seymour. "The Debate Within." *The New Yorker*, March 11, 2002.

Hoagland, Jim. "How CIA's Secret War on Saddam Collapsed." *Washington Post*, June 26, 1997.

Ignatius, David. "Letting Iraq Save Itself." *Washington Post*, September 5, 2003.

Indyk, Martin. "Back to the Bazaar." *Foreign Affairs* (January/February 2002).

King Jr., Neil. "Bush Officials Draft Broad Plan for Free-Market Economy in Iraq." *Wall Street Journal*, May 1, 2003.

MacFarquhar, Neil. "Rising Tide of Islamic Militants See Iraq as Ultimate Battlefield." *New York Times*, August 13, 2003.

McCarthy, Rory. *Guardian*, September 1, 2003.

Monderer, Michael and David Mulford. "Iraqi Debt, Like War, Divides the West." *Financial Times*, June 23, 2003.

Nakash, Yitzhak. "The Shi'ites and the Future of Iraq." *Foreign Affairs* 82: 4 (July/August 2003).

Powell, Colin L. "Remarks at the Elliot School of International Affairs." George Washington University, Washington, DC, September 5, 2003.

President George W. Bush. "Address to the Nation." Washington, DC, September 7, 2003, at <http://www.whitehouse.gov/news/releases/2003/09/print/20030907-1.html>

S/Res/1483, May 22, 2003.

Sanders, Edmund and Chris Kraul. "Bombing Disrupts Flow of Oil." *Los Angeles Times*, August 17, 2003.

Schweid, Barry. "Rumsfeld Rules Out Religious Iraqi Government." Associated Press Online, April 25, 2003.

Shadid, Anthony. "Iraqi Clerics Unite in Rare Alliance." *Washington Post*, August 17, 2003.

Shahzad, Syed Saleem. "A Third Force Awaits US in Iraq." *Asia Times*, March 1, 2003.

Slevin, Peter and Vernon Loeb. "Bremer: Iraq Effort to Cost Tens of Billions." *Washington Post*, August 27, 2003.

Stern, Jessica. "How America Created a Terrorist Haven." *New York Times*, August 20, 2003.

Taylor, John B. Under-Secretary for International Affairs, Department of the Treasury. Testimony before Senate Foreign Relations Committee, June 4, 2003.

Terrill, Andrew W. "Nationalism, Sectarianism, and the Future of the U.S. Presence in Post-Saddam Iraq." *Strategic Studies Institute* monograph 37 (July 2003).

Tierney, John. "A Popular Idea: Give Oil Money to the People Rather Than the Despots." *New York Times*, September 10, 2003.

Vieth, Warren. "U.S. to Let Iraq Manage Its Oil." *Los Angeles Times*, August 18, 2003.

Wolfowitz, Paul. Prepared Statement before Senate Armed Services Committee, September 9, 2003.

Zogby International. "The First Scientific Poll of Current Iraqi Public Opinion." *The American Enterprise*, August 2003.

INDEX